VENICE

D0008598

(Cover) Piazzetta San Marco, night view
Rio di Canonica

CONTENTS

St. Mark's Square, aerial view

H O W   T O   S E E   T H E

1 *ST. MARK'S BASILICA*

2 *DUCAL PALACE*

3 *PALAZZO REZZONICO*

4 *SCUOLA GRANDE OF SAN ROCCO*

5 *CHURCH OF S. MARIA
   GLORIOSA DEI FRARI*

6 *CA' D'ORO*

The numbers on the plan below correspond to those used in the itinerary. **1. St. Mark's Basilica** (page 38). Of special importance are: the mosaics, the Pala d'Oro. **2. Ducal Palace** (page 56). Of particular interest are: the Antechamber of the Hall of the Collegium, the Hall of the Collegium and the Great Council Hall; the statues of Adam and Eve. Proceed to the water-bus stop of S. Marco, and buy a ticket to Palazzo Rezzonico. The water-bus (vaporetto)

4

passes every 10 minutes. **3. Palazzo Rezzonico** (page 118). A magnificent example of an 18th. century Venetian patrician residence. The Church of S. Maria Gloriosa dei Frari should be visited before mid-day. **4. Scuola Grande of San Rocco** (page 124). Contains the most interesting of Jacopo Tintoretto's paintings. **5. Church of S. Maria Gloriosa dei Frari** (page 122). "The Assumption" by Titian. After visiting the Frari make for the Rialto on foot or by water-bus. There is time to stroll through the Rialto market and have lunch before visiting Cà d'Oro. **6. Cà d'Oro** (page 93). The house of a Venetian merchant in the Middle Ages. Retrace your steps to the Rialto and proceed to St. Mark's along the Mercerie. Once at St. Mark's it is time to have a rest, sit for a while at a table of one of the cafés in the Square, and watch the play of the afternoon sun on the mosaics of the basilica.

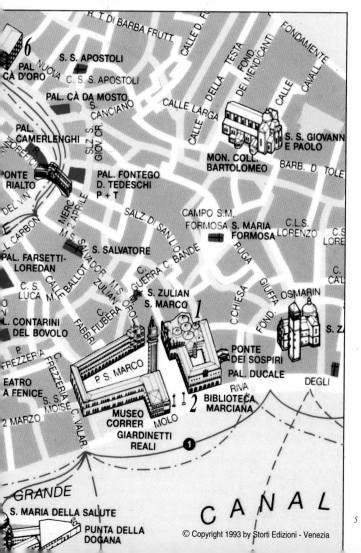

VENICE

◄ *St. Mark's Basin with the Library and the Basilica of the Salute*

THE PILINGS

The originality and the peculiarity of Venice arise principally from the natural setting of the city itself, built as it is on land which only just breaks the surface of the lagoon. These islands are made up of layers of differing kinds of soil, but the upper layers of silt were in any case unable to support the weight of buildings. Before beginning construction of a building it was therefore necessary to carry out consolidation work. This was achieved by driving piles into the earth and laying on them a platform of thick wooden planks. An excellent example of the process can be found in the description of the foundations of the church of S. Maria della Salute given in "Venezia, città nobilissima del Sansovino", published in Venice in 1663. "Construction was begun by driving into the subsoil one million, one hundred and six thousand six hundred and fifty-seven piles of oak, alder and larch, each about four metres long. This preparatory phase took about two years and two months to complete. Then a platform like a huge raft made of planks of oak and larch firmly lashed together was built on this base of piles".

Grand Canal. Rialto Bridge

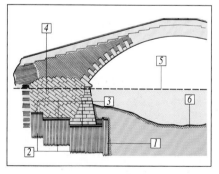

Constructional diagram of the foundations of the Rialto Bridge taken from "Il Campanile di San Marco, riedificato", published by the Venice City Council in 1912. 1- Piles of a bulkhead constructed to hold back the waters of the canal so that a dry area could be exposed for the laying of the foundations. 2- The six thousand piles which hold up the "Zatterone" or foundation platform. 3- The platform itself. 4- Masonry. 5- Average water level. 6- Bottom of the canal.

STYLES IN VENICE

As a result of its geographical position, of the way it developed over the centuries and of the lack of any strong classical tradition, the art and culture of Venice up to the 12th./13th. centuries remained essentially Byzantine, witness the greatest of all the city's religious buildings, the Basilica of St. Mark's. A few unmistakable basic elements identify Byzantine style : rounded, stilted arches, with later examples assuming an undulating horseshoe shape; capitals decorated with elegant relief engravings of leaves and symmetrical, matching figures; colourful marble-work. Romanesque style , with its simple rounded arches and thick, solid supporting walls which was typical of 12th. and 13th. century buildings, never really harmonized with the spirit and true nature of the city. The Ducal Palace, the most important Venetian public building and a classic symbol of Venice's beauty, was built in Gothic style . The fundamental unit from which the Venetian palace developed was the Byzantine warehouse - a one-storey building with a spacious portico and loggia. The Venetian palace retained the ground floor portico and first floor loggia and it is from this base that the walls rise faced with fine marble and crowned with pinnacles tipped with marble spheres to give a lightness to the whole. The ogival (pointed) arch assumes many different forms in Venice with the result that its basic function,

which was to take the weight of the downward thrust of the building, is forgotten in the general sense of decorative exuberance. The essential sympathy of Gothic style with the qualities of light and water which characterize Venice soon became apparent and the city took on a clear and original Gothic stamp which has lasted right up to the present day. The Renaissance 3 coincided with Venice's century of greatest splendour - the 15th. century. Architecture during the Renaissance in Venice often imposed rather heavy classical forms on the city and the influence of Michelangelo was felt. But it was rather in the decoration of ceilings, vaults and walls that Renaissance style made its finest contributions, and that because it was more in keeping with the established local traditions in these fields. Rather than the rounded arches, the orders and the proportions which governed the delineation of space, it was the new spirit with which these elements were manipulated which characterized the essence of Renaissance influence. In the 17th. century the Baroque, which was always prone to over-decoration in its attempt to harness the chromatic possibilities of movement, left one masterpiece in the church of S. Maria della Salute and then declined into even greater exaggeration and over-burdening of the decorative element. In the 18th. and 19th. centuries the Neo-classical movement rose to primacy and devoted itself primarily to the restoration and protection of Venice's incomparable artistic heritage.

Ducal Palace. Facade, a foreshortening

These walks help the visitor to get to know the city, with its lanes, bridges, religious buildings and houses. This is a way of seeing all the aspects of life in Venice, and it is left up to the visitor to pick out what he finds most interesting. Venice is a truly extraordinary city. It was the most important market centre in the Mediterranean in the 12th., 13th. and 14th. centuries, a link between east and west. Its inhabitants created a special civilisation, as we can admire in the churches, museums and galleries. The layout of the town reflects a way of life organised around its maritime location, with restricted spaces, narrow lanes, canals everywhere, some broad, some narrow, with the Grand Canal, the most imposing of all, few open spaces, with life set around the main centres - Rialto, St. Mark's and the Arsenal, all facing the sea. Due to the type of territory - small islands and sandbanks - the need to strengthen the foundations of the buildings with wooden piles, the corrosion with which these are threatened and the movement of the waters, the architects have always tried to limit the weight of the walls with spacious openings and by using bricks. This means that there is no monumental architecture in Venice, but there are marble decorated rows of windows and inner and outer mosaic embellishments. The walks we suggest will help you approach this situation, the unique and incomparable result of the efforts of man and nature.

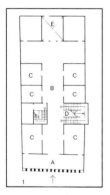

Civil Architecture. The ancient tradition in civil architecture dates back to the period of trade exchange between Venice and Byzantium. Architectural distribution of the different parts of the house makes provision for long, spacious rooms, lending themselves to the transfer and storage of goods. Due to the particular attributes of available building land the Venetians saw the Byzantine fondaco, a street-level dwelling serving as both warehouse and office premises, as a suitable building model.

Cà Corner Loredan, ground-floor plan. A *Portico.* B *Hall.* C *Store-rooms.* D *Stairs.* E *Garden.*

Church Architecture. The architectural evolution of church building in Venice springs initially from the Cathedral of S. Maria Assunta on the island of Torcello. A typical 11th. century Veneto-Byzantine structure, the church in all probability differs little from the first building erected on the site (639) see p.128. The cathedral plan is of the Roman basilican type, with a broad central nave and two narrow aisles, choir and iconostasis, 7th. century high altar, presbytery with steps and bishops's throne.

Plan of the Cathedral of Torcello. A *Iconostasis.* B *High Altar.* C *Presbytery.* D *Chair.*

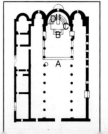

1 - Tronchetto (car and coach park) - Piazzale Roma - Tolentini - Scuola Grande of San Rocco (page 124) - Frari Church (page 122) - Embarkation for St. Mark's at San Tomà (see page 4)

2 - St. Mark's Square (page 28) - Mercerie - Church of San Zulian (page 104) - Church of Santa Maria Formosa (page 104) - Church of Saints John and Paul (page 106) - Church of Santa Maria dei Miracoli (page 105) - Rialto Bridge (page 89)

3 - St. Mark's Square (page 28) - Riva degli Schiavoni (page 72) - Church of San Zaccaria (page 110) - Rio di San Lorenzo - School of San Giorgio degli Schiavoni (page 109) - Arsenal Museum (page 108) - (Vaporetto for St. Mark's)

4 - St. Mark's Square (page 28) - Contarini dal Bovolo Palace (page 103) - Calle della Mandola - Church of S. Stefano (page 102) - Accademia Gallery (page 96) - Zattere - Basilica della Salute (page 82) - (Vaporetto St. Mark's, line 1)

5 - Railway station - Lista di Spagna - Ghetto (page 113) - Strada Nuova - Church of Santi Apostoli (page 112) - Mercerie - St. Mark's (page 28)

6 - Rialto Bridge (page 89) - Campo S. Polo - San Tomà - San Pantalon - Campo Santa Margherita - Palazzo Rezzonico (page 118) - Accademia Gallery (page 96) - Guggenheim Collection (page 83) - Basilica della Salute (page 82) - St. Mark's (page 28)

The Campanile seen from the arcade of the Ducal Palace

VENICE

The Veneti, who by the 13th. century had achieved so much in terms of social values, eight centuries previously were only just beginning to emerge onto the stage of history. They lived, fearful and forlorn in an ill-defined triangle of land the base of which was formed by the River Po and the sides by the Adriatic Sea and the Alps. The northern-most tip of the triangle was defended by the fortress of Aquileia. Some inhabited cities already boasted a long tradition - Padua, Altino, Oderzo, Concordia, Aquileia - and devoted themselves to agriculture and horse-breeding as well as to the manufacture of weaponry and glass. Others lived in forgotten little villages scattered along the coast fishing and manufacturing salt. The region is crossed by the Rivers Brenta, Piave, Livenza and Tagliamento and at the point at which they meet the sea form extensive lagoons.

In the 5th. century, the barbarians found that their easiest route from the North to Rome lay through these parts. First Aquileia was destroyed by Attila in 453, and subsequently the whole of the territory of the Veneti was gradually burnt and sacked as the barbarians increased their attacks on the capital of the Empire. The inhabitants of the zone took refuge amongst the islands of the lagoon. At first, when the destructive wave of barbarians had passed through, the Veneti tended to return to their home towns, but when once again they were threatened, this time by the Lombards during the 7th. century, the retreat to their refuges on the islands of the lagoon was final, and the communities of Chioggia, Malamocco, Jesolo, Eraclea, Caorle and Grado were established to take the place of the unsafe mainland towns. The refugees constructed their own flat-bottomed boats for moving about in the shallow waters of the lagoon, huts mounted on piles, and ground-floor rooms in stone which they brought with them from the mainland together with their livestock and their religious and civil traditions. These lagoon-dwellers found themselves under the sway of Byzantium and in order to survive, had to defend themselves from the attacks of barbarians from the mainland and of pirates from the sea. In 697, the representative of the Byzantine Empire at Ravenna appointed Paoluccio Anafesto as "Dux" - a kind of military leader - for the inhabitants of the lagoons, and some degree of autonomy was granted to certain of the island communities. Before long two settlements began to emerge as more important than the others - Grado established itself as the religious, and Eraclea as the political centre, though the latter was subsequently replaced by Malamocco which, in its turn, was destroyed by the sea. Torcello meanwhile established itself as a commercial centre of some importance. The Franks, having first subjugated the Lombards, attempted also to defeat the lagoon communities by simultaneously mounting an attack from the mainland and also an encircling movement along the neck of land on the seaward side of the lagoon. In 809, Pippin, the son of Charlemagne, pushed so far along the littoral that the liberty of the Veneti was seriously threatened. Faced with this common danger, the lagoon communities decided to join forces, and in an attempt to put an end to the hostilities which existed between them, established a completely new, central political headquarters at Rivus Altus - deep water, Rialto - and a single new religious centre. In 829, two merchants, Buono of Malamocco and Rustico of Torcello, smuggled the body of St. Mark the Evangelist out of Alexandria in Egypt, and brought it to Rialto.

Early constructions at Rialto

Such decisions as these made quite clear the determination of the Veneti to live as free men, rejecting even dominion by Byzantium. St. Mark, the new patron saint of the city, took the place of the Greek St. Theodore. Throughout the two hundred years between 800 and 1000 the Veneti continued to pursue a political course based on the protection of their liberty and independence even though this policy at times brought them to the brink of disaster. In order to neutralize the threat from the barbarians who held the mainland, the Veneti purged the ranks of their governing class of all Frankish sympathizers, and in an attempt to protect their seaward flank they made an alliance with Byzantium against the pirates of the Adriatic and against the Saracens and the Normans. In the year 1000 Pietro Orseolo II won a notable victory against the pirates on Ascension Day- "il giorno della Sensa". This prudent and courageous political move at one stroke consolidated their prestige, obtained special privileges from the Byzantines and ensured the enforcement of their authority over the other peoples who inhabited the Adriatic coasts. The Dux of Rialto which was still the name of the city, became also Dux of Dalmatia.

High Water. The waters that flood nearly all of this town now and then during October, November and December, cause serious damage and are a risk to the stability of the buildings. The causes of this phenomenon are the adverse meteorological conditions - the wind blowing in from the east -, the

St. Mark's Square with
the Basin. Aerial view

Piazzetta San Marco. High Water

filling up of large areas of the lagoon, the slow submergence of the city, the
transformation of some of the canals with the overturning of the natural
flow of the currents coming in from the sea and the significant difference
between high and low tide.

The development of the city. By the 11th. century the appearance of the lagoon had changed. The edges of the islands had been consolidated, new canals had been excavated and others filled in to facilitate communications. The area of the Rialto was the scene of brisk community life and was also the site of the residence of the Dux. This "Cason" or large house was built with stones and bricks from Torcello where houses had been demolished. Everywhere could be seen wooden houses built on piles, with spacious, brick-built rooms on the ground floor where people lived together with their livestock and merchandise. Many people were involved in the salt manufacturing industry sited at various points along the edges of the canals; others worked at the water-driven grain mills or constructed or repaired boats in the squeri (boatyards). On the swampy grounds of the Monastery of San Zaccaria, between the ancient chapel of St. Theodore and the new castle of the Dux, a new church to St. Mark was being built. On the edge of the Batario Canal in front of the church a look-out tower was raised to complete the defence system which also included St. George, the Punta della Dogana and the church of S. Maria Zobenigo. Access to the Grand Canal was prevented by chains. The life of the community was regulated by the ringing of the bells of the churches and monasteries as they summoned the people to religious services, to public meetings in the muddy spaces before the churches to witness judgements and executions to hear laws promulgated and government decisions announced. **Doge Sebastiano Ziani.** Amongst the events which can be cited as examples of the increasingly important role being played in history by the Veneti were the mission as mediator in the struggle between Pope Alexander III and Frederick Barbarossa entrusted to the Doge Sebastiano Ziani (1172-1178), the conquest of Constantinople in 1202-1204 and the defeat of Genoa in 1378. Meanwhile, there began those events in which the whole population participated year after year both as protagonist and as spectators: the Spring day when the galleys left on their trade voyages saw everyone out along the banks to see them off for example, and again to greet them on their return in Autumn; then there was enthusiastic mass participation at the festivals surrounding the annual ceremonies of the Marriage with the Sea on Ascension Day - the "Sensa" - and the "Marie". If the "Sensa" was a celebration of national heroism, the festival of the "Marie" commemorated the valour of the people of Rialto: during a marriage ceremony at the church of S. Pietro di Castello, a band of pirates had burst into the church and kidnapped and carried off the brides-to-be. Their young suitors gave chase, put the pirates to the sword and returned home triumphantly with their women-folk. The episode came to symbolize the courage and strength of the peoples of the lagoon.

Ducal Palace. Jacopo Palma the Younger, The Conquest of Constantinople

The Crusades and Constantinople. The Crusades were at the same time the most emblematic and the most revolutionary of mediaeval movements, from the point of view both of the ideas which gave them birth and therefore sustained them and also of the changes which they brought about in feudal society. The marine republics of the peninsula - Genoa, Pisa and Rialto - were all anxious to exploit the commercial advantages the Crusades could bring them. At the beginning, Rialto held aloof from the expeditions in order to protect the position of special privilege she enjoyed at Byzantine ports; but as soon as she realized what immense benefits the transport of crusaders was bringing her rivals, she quickly joined in and as a result of her part in the formidable organization and execution in the Fourth Crusade, achieved dominion over "a quarter and a half of the Empire of Constantinople." It was the year 1204 in Constantinople a city now conquered by the Venetians and Crusaders. A month has already passed since Enrico Dandolo, preceded only by his ensign, leaped to land before the unassailable walls of the city. At the sight of the octogenarian Doge of Rialto alone in the face of the gun-fire and arrows, the soldiers launched a furious attack at the walls and poured into the city overcoming every effort of the defenders to repel them. In no time at all the city had been reduced to a pile of rubble, the walls dismantled, the streets filled with refuse, the churches profaned. The Crusaders who set out to free the Holy Sepulchre in Jerusalem now roam the streets of the capital of the Eastern Roman Empire thirsting for blood and greedy for plunder. The Greeks who managed to survive massacre hide in horrified terror. In the area known as Galata, the free port of the Venetians, all seems quiet and under control, and the space in front of the residence of the Doge is well defended by guards. This very morning, at a meeting of the leaders of the Crusade, Enrico Dandolo refused their offer of the title of Emperor, insisting instead that the pacts sworn by them all at the church of St. Mark two years before be honoured: the Crusaders must now pay in gold and silver the price 19

Correr Museum. The badge of the barbers' trade

agreed for transporting the expedition. Moreover, the aged but tenacious Doge demanded trading privileges and landing rights for the galleys of his city in all the ports of the Eastern Mediterranean. At the end of the meeting he took the place of the Papal Legate and himself placed the imperial crown on the head of Baldwin of Flanders. This final act of the Fourth Crusade ensured for Venice a predominant position throughout the entire Mediterranean. Enrico Dandolo might well be taken as a symbol of the Venetian: tempered in the struggle against the sea and for mastery of the sea; a shrewd businessman and able to drive a hard bargain; relentless in the pursuit of his target: proud of his native city and ready to make any sacrifice for her; a profoundly religious man, though gifted with brilliant open-mindedness, in-built as the result of a heritage of centuries of contact with peoples of all races and creeds. **Venice and Genoa**. The Fourth Crusade however was only one episode in the centuries-long struggle between Venice and Genoa for supremacy in the Mediterranean. The struggle was punctuated by battles from which either one or the other of the contenders emerged as victor, and after each battle followed a period of peace which lasted just long enough for wounds to be licked and repairs and preparations made for the next battle at which each would be once again determined to annihilate the other. The decisive battle took place at Chioggia at the southern edge of the lagoon, almost within sight of the horses which had been placed on the facade of the Basilica of St. Mark as a symbol of power and freedom. The Commander of the Genoese fleet, confident that he was about to drown the city of Venice in its own waters, refused the peace offer made to him by the Venetian forces. So sure was he of victory that he declared that he would agree to peace "only after he had bridled the horses of St. Mark." As matters turned out, the Venetians summoned all the necessary reserves of strength and at the battle of Chioggia completely destroyed the Genoese fleet and put an end once and for all to Genoa's ambitions.

St. Mark's and the Rialto. With Constantinople conquered and domination of the whole of the Mediterranean achieved, the Venetian galleys now returned home laden with riches, with merchandise of every conceivable kind - gold, spices, silks, brocades and works of art. Rialto - Venice - it was around this time that the city finally took its present name - was the most congested port in the Mediterranean. The Palace and the Chapel of the Doges underwent radical changes. After successive fires and pillagings the Doge's Chapel (the Basilica of St. Mark) finally assumed the noble architectural form that we now know. The raising of the two great columns in the Piazzetta was a great public occasion and when a third column slipped beneath the waters of the lagoon taking with it sailors and workmen, a grief-stricken silence fell over the watching crowd as they experienced a common sense of tragedy. When the golden horses were set in place on the facade of the church, their age and beauty aroused intense interest and admiration. And the pose of these sculptures, caught at full gallop with the excitement of unrestrained and unrestrainable forward impetus coursing throught their limbs, became the symbol of the supreme liberty of the city. The Arsenal, sited as if to defend the city, now took over most of the productive capacity of the "squeri" or private boat-yards. In the 13th. century, boats were being made and launched at the rate of one a day and always to patterns laid down by the government; this last measure so that in case of necessity the maximum number of craft could be converted into galleys or other war-ships. The Venetian merchant was also commander of his trading fleet. The area around the oldest church of Rialto (S. Giacomo; 451) developed into the commercial centre of the city. The ferry across the Grand Canal at this point soon proved unable to cope with the demand so the government had a draw-bridge built. Anyone looking down the Grand Canal at that time would have seen heavy cargo ships anchored in front of the one storey buildings which lined the banks. Behind and clustered around these more substantial buildings could be seen the damp and musty huts of the boat-men and the salt workers. A narrow muddy lane led from the new Rialto Bridge to St. Mark's where rough-looking Slavs and Scandinavians mingled with refined Greeks and Levantines with their perfumed garments, and over all the cosmopolitan crowd stood the figure of Venice.

The Ducal Palace.
Paolo Veronese,
The Battle of Chioggia

The Government of the City-State. The following is an outline of the government institutions which developed in Venice over the centuries. At the head of the various institutions which made up the "Most Serene Republic" - "La Serenissima" - stood the Dux and he held the title of "Principe Serenissimo". He was always patrician and was elected for life by his peers, the other Venetian nobles. Executive power rested with the Dux together with an inner council of state known as the Signoria. The voice of the people was officially heard through the Great Council or the Council of the Five Hundred. The Dux was entitled, if he saw fit, to call another Council of "Pregadi" or "invited ones"which was also known as the Senate. In 1297, the Dux Pietro Gradenigo managed to get a law passed by which the common people were excluded from the affairs of government, an event which became known as the "lock-out of the Great Council". The first half of the 14th. century was one of the most delicate periods in Venetian history. With Gradenigo's law considerable discontent smouldered among the common people and this erupted in two revolts - the first in 1300 led by Marin Bocconio and the second in 1310, led by Baiamonte Tiepolo. Later, in 1355, Marin Faliero attempted to seize power from the government but this, like all the other attempts at revolt, was quickly crushed and the patricians tightened their grip on the reins of government. Indeed, in order to further ensure continuation of the power and privileges which they had accumulated over the years, the nobles instituted a new, supreme State Tribunal, known as the Council of Ten. With Marco Polo, pioneer merchant and diplomat, and protagonist of a thousand adventures which he tried in vain to convince his contemporaries were true, the period which began with the exploits of Enrico Dandolo draws to a close.

Francesco Foscari. At the apex of Venice's period of political, military and economic greatness stands the long reign of the Doge Francesco Foscari from 1423 to 1457. Other events of this period - the fall of Constantinople in 1453 and the arrival of Vasco da Gama in the Indies in 1498 - mark the moment of the transformation of this greatness into the different splendour of artistic and social greatness. Foscari's policy was to counter-balance the loss of territory and markets in the Eastern Mediterranean by changing Venice into a mainland power. Venice extended its dominion over the Veneto and into Lombardy and thus managed to lessen the commercial threat which competition from these states represented, but on the other hand she incurred the enmity of the Pope and other states of the peninsula and was now forced to withdraw from the sea which was not only her natural element but also the traditional source of her power and wealth.

Grand Canal. Palazzi Balbi, Foscari, Giustinian, Rezzonico

Venice takes on her present appearance. Despite naval setbacks and her continuing withdrawal from the seas of the Eastern Mediterranean, Venice and her government still enjoyed a certain prestige. The nobles however, less involved in the direction of the political and economic affairs of state, dedicated themselves increasingly to the arts and literature. After the fall of Constantinople, Venice gradually changed into a cultural and artistic centre. Aldus Manutius and Cardinal Bessarion, the Raverti and the Bon families, Sansovino and Palladio, the Bellini and Vivarini families, Mantegna and Carpaccio and later Giorgione, Titian, Tintoretto and Veronese were the printers, scholars, sculptors, architects and painters who celebrated the magnificence of Venice through their art. And it was around this time that Venice took on the appearance we know today. St. Mark's Square was enlarged to its present size and shape, the Campanile was isolated from other buildings as it is now, and the church of S. Geminiano was constructed at the far end of the square opposite the Basilica. The square took its shape from the rhythmically flowing lines of the Procuratie, and the Piazzetta from the construction of the Libreria. Two - and three - storey palaces began to take up all available space along the banks of the Grand Canal, while at Rialto a stone bridge was built to take the place of the rickety wooden one. The people still devoted some time and effort to trade and fishing but increasingly important was the work of building; using the stocks of wood which were daily unloaded from the large rafts along the wharves of the Zattere. New buildings crowded in on the narrow streets and the canals were increasingly blocked by their burden of rubble: and over this forest of new buildings watched 150 church bell-towers.

The Centuries of Decline. Political relations between Venice and the Papacy continued to worsen until the Interdict (Paolo Sarpi: 1606) while Spain resorted even to betrayal in its attempts to conquer the city (Bedmar: 1618). The defeat suffered by the Turks at the Battle of Lepanto (1571) did little to stop them continuing to conquer ports and possessions in the Eastern Mediterranean which had belonged to Venice. Now cut off from the great trade routes, Venice made what pacts she could in order to retain those territories which had not already been lost. In the naval battles fought to contain the irresistible advance of the Turks, certain of the Venetian nobles covered themselves with glory; Tommaso Mocenigo, Lorenzo Marcello, Francesco Morosini (1699) made great names for themselves but nevertheless failed to obtain lasting results, still less to change the course of events. On the 12th. May, 1797, Ludovico Manin, the hundred and twentieth Doge of the Serenissima Republic handed over power in the city to the French. Later the same year at Campoformido, Napoleon ceded Venice and its territories to Austria. The city was to remain in the hands of the Austrians through the revolution of 1848-1849 until 1866 when the

populace voted that Venice should join the Kingdom of Italy. The city in which the cycle of 1000 years of independence thus came to a close looked more or less as it does today. Churches and palaces, hovels and pile-dwellings, vast garden areas, lanes choked with goods and shaded by awnings. The immense Square, full of pedlar's stalls, puppet showmen and soothsayers. Many were the theatres, gaming rooms and holidays. The patricians were victims of a stylized way of life, practically frozen in an unreal world. During the Napoleonic era, amongst other things the four horses of St. Mark's were taken to Paris, the church of S. Geminiano was demolished, several canals were filled in and the areas of Via Garibaldi and S. Elena were established. Under the Austrians, the four horses were returned to the Basilica and the bridge at the Accademia and the causeway to the mainland were built. Above and beyond the realm of historical events, the city of Venice can be considered as an experiment carried out by man, and seen in this light, the city belongs to man, to all humanity. And humanity thus has a duty to preserve this irreplaceable part of its own past, of its own identity.

Accademia Gallery. Gentile Bellini,
Procession in St. Mark's Square

ITIN

VENICE

A Canal with a gondola

Piazzetta San Marco.
The gondola station

3

ACCADEMIA
GALLERY

CAMPO SANTO STEFANO

CHURCH OF SAN MOISE'

St. Mark's Basin. Sunset

6

PALAZZO REZZONICO

CHURCH OF S. MARIA
GLORIOSA DEI FRARI

SCUOLA GRANDE
OF SAN ROCCO

ST. MARK'S SQUARE
ST. MARK'S BASILICA
THE DUCAL PALACE

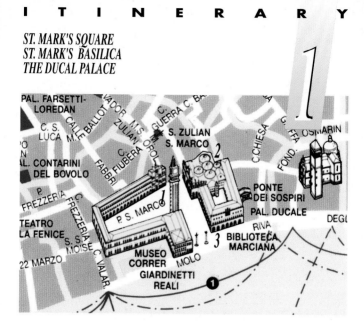

1-St. Mark's Square. 2-St. Mark's Basilica. 3-Ducal Palace

ST. MARK'S SQUARE

During the period of the Serenissima Republic, St. Mark's Square was the political and religious centre of the city while the Rialto was its commercial heart. Nowadays the Square is recognized the world over as one of the symbols of the city's beauty. In the year 1000, the site was occupied by a vegetable garden cut in two by the Batario Canal and with the Churches of St. Mark on one side and of S. Geminiano on the other. Over the following centuries the future square was gradually marked out by the houses built for the chaplains of St. Mark's and palaces for the Procurators who were state magistrates with representative functions, hence the name Procuratie. The Campanile, originally a lighthouse and lookout tower was raised to its present height only in the 16th. century. Already in Gentile Bellini's "Procession in St. Mark's Square" (1496), which can now be seen at the Accademia Gallery, the Byzantine buildings with their crenellations surround the square and the campanile is built into one of the wings of these palaces. At the beginning of the Renaissance and then throughout the 16th. century, the square underwent considerable changes. Mauro Coducci constructed the Procuratie Vecchie on the right hand side (15th.-16th. centuries), and also, with Pietro Lombardo, the Clock Tower (15th.-16th. centuries). The Procuratie Nuove were built on the left by Vincenzo Scamozzi in the 16th. century, but it was not until the 19th. century that the Procuratie Nuovissime were built to the orders of Napoleon after the church of S. Geminiano had been demolished.

28

The Clock Tower. The Clock Tower was built to complete the view of the square from the Basin of St. Mark's and to join the line of the Procuratie Vecchie to the buildings in the space beside the Basilica of St. Mark's. It is a decorative element which blends perfectly into the surrounding architecture. At the top of the Tower stand two bronze statues - the "Mori" or Moors - who strike the hours. On the front of the tower several details, both decorative and functional may be seen: the signs of the zodiac, the clock face itself and the winged lion, the symbol of the city. During the week around Ascension day and at Epiphany statues of the three Magi appear from inside the Clock Tower, bow their homage to the Virgin and retire.

The Clock Tower. Night view   *St. Mark's Square* ▶

Clock Tower. The two Moors striking the hour

The Clock Tower. Detail

The Campanile of St. Mark's. The brickbuilt bell-tower reaches a height of 98,60 metres. There are small windows all the way up the side and the belfry itself is open. At the very top stands a gilded statue of an angel. In 1902 the campanile collapsed, but by 1912 it had been replaced by an identical copy. The bells all bear names which recall the function that they had when summoning the populace: la Marangona which announced starting and finishing times for guild workers; la Trottiera which bade nobles hurry to the Doge's Palace: la Nona which rang for mid-day; the Pregadi which announced meetings of the Senate; and the Renghiera or Maleficio which gave the signal that a capital execution was to take place.

The Loggetta. The Loggetta - a small loggia - had a function very similar to others of its kind: it offered a suitable space for meetings and discussions and was sometimes used as a guard post. The Loggetta was constructed by Jacopo Sansovino and the whole building acquires its special character from the elegant sculptures which adorn its facade. The bronze gates were cast in the 18th. century by Antonio Gai.

The Loggetta by Jacopo Sansovino

The Piazzetta. The Piazzetta is the space bordered by the Doge's Palace, the Library and the South facade of the Basilica. The two massive columns which mark its edge on the lagoon side were brought there from the Eastern Mediterranean in the 12th. century and now bear the two symbols of the city, the lion of St. Mark and the statue of St. Theodore. Over the centuries the Piazzetta was witness to many of the ceremonial occasions which punctuated the life of Venetians such as the departure and arrival of the city's fleets, official processions, festive occasions such as Carnival, and capital executions.

Saint Mark's Square. Aerial view

Piazzetta San Marco and the Clock Tower in the background
Grand Canal, night view

St. Mark's Basilica,
narthex.
The Tower of Babel (mosaic)

Piazzetta San Marco. The Marciana Library

The Library. The Library was built by Jacopo Sansovino in the 16th. century. This masterpiece of the Renaissance is distinguished by the supreme balance and harmony of its component parts - arches, architraves and the crowning statues. The atrium and the great hall inside are decorated with canvases by various artists including Titian, Tintoretto and Veronese, and the spacious library itself contains the superb collection of the Biblioteca Marciana including such rare books as the famous Grimani Breviary. **The Archeological Museum**. On display in the museum are various statues and coins from the Greco-Roman era and a few fragments of Egyptian and Assyrian and Babylonian sculpture. **Correr Museum**. The collection of the museum is displayed in rooms on the first and second floors of the Procuratie Nuove. The entrance is in the Procuratie Nuovissime. The first floor is dedicated to relics of the period of the Serenissima Republic and the collection of prints of views of Venice down the centuries. The collection of paintings is well displayed on the second floor and includes Carpaccio's famous painting entitled "The Courtesans" as well as a "Christ with Angels" by Antonello da Messina, a "Pietà" by Cosmè Tura and three canvases by Giovanni Bellini - a "Crucifixion", a "Transfiguration" and a "Madonna and Child".

ST. MARK'S BASILICA

Over the centuries of the Serenissima Republic, the Basilica of St. Mark represented a reference point both political and religious for the citizens of Venice. From the moment it was established in the 9th. century to house the body of St. Mark which had been smuggled out of Alexandria to take the place of the Greek saint, Theodore, the building served to emphasize Venice's break with the Emperor at Byzantium and to accentuate the city's independence in religious as well as political matters. As time went on the significance which the people and government of Venice had deliberately attributed to St. Mark's was consolidated and reinforced and as the Doge's Chapel, it was covered with gold and pearls and works of art of inestimable value. Then, as soon as possible, those symbols of the freedom and independence of the city, the four horses, were set in their commanding place on the facade of the church.

St. Mark's Basilica, the west or main facade. Upper section

The innumerable statues of saints, both inside and outside the building, make quite clear the extraordinary influence which St. Mark's exerted over the spirits of Venetians in both religious and political matters. The first religious building on this site was a chapel constructed to house the body of St. Mark in the 9th. century. This chapel was destroyed by fire and was replaced by another in the 10th. century. The second building, in wood, also fell an easy prey fo flames and was replaced by the present building which was begun in the 11th. century. Built on the plan of a Greek cross the three arms of the cross are surrounded by a narthex which is interrupted on the right hand side.

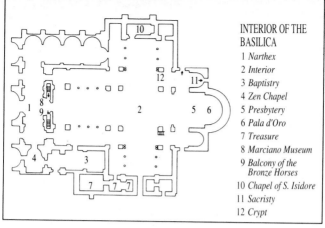

Plan of St. Mark's Basilica

St. Mark's Basilica ►

The exterior facades show traces of several different architectural styles - Byzantine, Romanesque and Gothic - and are interrupted by a wide balcony. On the great balcony of the main facade above the principal entrance to the basilica can be seen the Four Horses which were taken from the Hippodrome in Byzantium in 1204 and brought to Venice. The present state of our knowledge of the horses' history does not permit us to give a reliable date for their origin. The walls of the basilica are made of brick and covered with marble slabs and a large number of columns. The arches are decorated with mosaics which show the journey of the relics of St. Mark from Alexandria to Venice.

St. Mark's Basilica, main portal. The upper part

The oldest mosaic, which dates from the 13th. century, can be seen in the first archway from the left. Around the main arch of the entrance is a remarkable decorative frieze, symbolic figures sculpted in Romanesque and Byzantine style in the 12th.-13th. centuries. Of particular interest are the figures representing the months and the crafts - their Romanesque origins are clear from both form and iconography. The upper lunettes contain mosaics whose subjects are the principal festivals of the Church. Anyone looking at the facade of the Basilica from the Square will notice how like a huge altar it is, an impression which creates a remarkable sense of unity and continuity between exterior and interior. Moreover,the compactness of the Square undeniably lends it a function of peoples' cloister or church. The Proclamation Stone (Pietra del Bando) stands next to the right hand corner of the Basilica. The Narthex or Atrium is the space within the walls of the church and on the same level as the Square. It gives the impression of being a continuation of the Square though in fact it is already part of the Basilica itself. The cupolas of the Narthex are low, windowless and fairly shallow, and are decorated with mainly 13th. century mosaics which deal with episodes from the Old Testament such as the Creation, Noah, The Tower of Babel, Abraham, Joseph and Moses. Beautiful too are the 12th.-13th. century mosaic floors and the fine columns which adorn the walls. The Narthex with its soft, restrained light, calls the worshipper to a moment of pause, of meditation to prepare the spirit before entering the church. To reach the level of the church itself, the visitor must go up first five and then another two steps - seven in all. The interior space is contained, measured by pillars, arches, cupolas. The mosaic floors, the elegant columns, the gilded capitals, the arches and golden cupolas all contribute to render the space even more open and extensive and to lighten the effect of the constructional materials. In the delicate half-light people seem to lose something of the distinctness of their shapes as if the individual were of little importance before the Divine.

St. Mark's Basilica, main facade.
The four horses in their traditional
position on the facade

The four horses
now in the
Marciano Museum

43

The Mosaics. The principal and most striking aspect of the interior of the Basilica is undoubtedly the mosaic decoration. The technique of mosaic decoration is relatively simple. Small cubes of glass or coloured stone which are called "tessere" are set in a substance which holds them in place. The "tessere" are of different colours and they may be set following a design which has either been traced directly onto the wall or onto a cartoon. Both these techniques were used in the Basilica, the first method being used for the oldest of the mosaics - those up to the 15th. century - and the second method for all subsequent mosaics. Another distinctive element of the Basilica derives from the fact that the mosaicists of the 11th. 12th. 13th. and 14th. centuries were all Greek and the style of each of these master craftsmen can be clearly identified according to the schools they came from. Gradually over the centuries, local craftsmen acquired the techniques from the Greek masters and examples of their work may be seen in the Baptistry and the Chapel of St. Isidore where the mosaics tell the story of the life and death of the saints. In the early years of the 15th. century the Greek master-craftsmen withdrew altogether and the local artists lost their creative impulse: it was in this period of crisis that the stylistic beginnings of the second phase have their origins. Famous painters such as Paolo Uccello and Andrea del Castagno began to arrive in Venice, and they prepared cartoons for the mosaics which cover the vault of the Mascoli Chapel and the great arch above the Gothic rose window of the right transept. Thenceforth mosaics were designed and set in place on all the walls which had not yet been decorated, but also, though some were restored, many of the mosaics which were crumbling were radically changed or replaced altogether.

St. Mark's Basilica. Central nave

St. Mark's Basilica, narthex.
Cupola of the Creation

*St. Mark's
Basilica, narthex.
Main Entrance,
mosaics.*

*St. Mark's
Basilica, apse.
Transport of St.
Mark's body
(mosaic)*

The following are the parts of the Basilica, together with their decorations, which are liturgically more important. The lunette above the main entrance. *The Deesis* or *The Saviour between the Virgin and St. Mark* (13th. century, restored). The First Cupola. *The Pentecost* (12th. century). The Holy Ghost descends on the Apostles in the form of tongues of fire. The wall of the right nave. *Christ among the Prophets* (Venetian school of the 13th. century). The wall above the Baptistry. *Jesus in the Garden* (13th. century). The great arch over the Baptistry. *Scenes from the life of Christ and of the Apostles Simon, Jude, Matthew, Philip and James the Less* (Venetian school of the 12th.-13th. centuries). The wall of the left nave. *The Virgin among the Prophets* (Venetian school of the 13th. century). The Arch between the First and Second Cupolas. *Scenes of the Passion* (13th. century). The dramatic tension of the groups and the stylization of the gestures betray the Romanesque origins of these mosaics. Second Cupola. *Ascension* (13th. century). The Ascension is the most emblematic event of the New Testament: the human form absorbed into the divine essence. Clear stylistic evidence of Byzantine and Romanesque influence. Cupola, left transept. The Fathers of the Church and the life of Saint John the Baptist (12th. century). Great arch over the nave of the left transept. *The life of the Virgin and the childhood of Christ* (12th-13th. centuries). Great arch over the Chapel of St. Isidore. *Events from the life of Christ* (12th.-13th. centuries). Cupola in the right transept. *Saints Nicholas, Clement, Blaise, and Leonard* and in the spandrels *Saints Erasmus, Dorothy, Euphemia and Thecla* (Venetian school of the 13th. century). The right wall of the right transept. *The finding of the body of St. Mark* (second half of the 13th. century). The left wall of the right transept. *Events from the life of Christ* (12th. and 13th. centuries). The Presbytery Cupola. *The Prophets announce Christ and His Religion*. This is one of the early mosaics and bears traces of the influence of Byzantium and Ravenna. It has been considerably restored. The Cove of the Apse. *Christ Enthroned* (remade in the 16th. century) and *Saints Hermagorus, Mark, Peter and Nicholas*. These mosaics were created in the time of Doge Domenico Selvo (1071-1084). The great arches on the right and left of the Presbytery, *Events from the life of St. Clement* and *the figures of Cain and Abel* (12th. century).

St. Mark's Basilica. Golden Altarpiece

Golden Altarpiece. Resurrection
Golden Altarpiece. Entrance into Jerusalem

The mosaic decoration of the Basilica covers the entire upper part of the church, the narthex, the chapels and the sacristy extending over a total area of 4000 square metres. Thus many of the mosaics belong to the period of the second style, and of these the "paintings in mosaic" of the sacristy and the great arches around the central cupola are particularly beautiful. The Pala d'Oro or **Golden Altarpiece** rises behind the main altar where the sarcophagus of St. Mark can be seen. With the mosaics this is the other decorative element which seems to bring together the various associations of the Golden Basilica. The Pala d'Oro, created by Giampaolo Bonisegna in the 14th. century, is a sumptuous example of the goldsmith's craft and of high artistic and spiritual value. It is rectangular in shape (3.48x1.40 metres), and is set with eighty enamelled tablets. Most of them are examples of extremely refined Byzantine art of the 10th. to the 13th. centuries, but there are also some examples of local Venetian art of the 13th. and 14th. centuries. In the Pala d'Oro are summed up not only the heroic exploits and economic and military conquests of this people of navigators and pioneers but also their spirit, their taste, their generosity and their faith.

St. Mark's Basilica. Baptistry

St. Mark's Basilica. Baptistry, The Dance of Salome

The **Baptistry**. The Baptistry was built into the right wing of the Narthex and is remarkable for the vigorous modelling of the figures in the mosaic decoration and the tombs, both of the 14th. century. The mosaics treat episodes from the Life of St. John the Baptist and from the Childhood of Christ. Above the entrance can be seen the Dance of Salome; the slender dancer in her rich, clinging dress sways together with other courtesans before Herod and his mother who are seated at a richly laid table. The scene is amongst the most richly evocative of the mosaics created in the 14th. century. The tombs of the Doges Andrea Dandolo and Giovanni Soranzo are set into the wall. The baptismal font is of the 16th. century and is surmounted by Francesco Segala's statue of St. John the Baptist. The altar is a massive piece of granite from which Jesus is said to have spoken to the multitudes. It was brought to the Basilica from Tyre in the 12th. century. The **Zen Chapel**. Before the creation of the chapel in the right hand corner of the Narthex in 1521, a great door gave access to and from the Piazzetta at this point. Space in the chapel is almost entirely taken up by the great, somewhat heavy bronze altar which bears the statue of the Madonna of the Shoe. The mosaics have the same stylistic characteristics as those in the Narthex but have been considerably restored. The **Treasury of St. Mark's**. Various attempts have been made over the centuries to find a permanent arrangement for the display of the Basilica's collection of precious objects and reliquaries, and the present site, in three rooms of the tower of the church which stands next to the Porta della Carta of the Doge's Palace, is still temporary. The precious objects and relics displayed are what remains of the priceless treasury which the Venetians accumulated during their centuries of voyaging. Though many pieces have been lost, the collection still boasts goblets, knives, crucifixes, chalices, thrones and altar screens of the highest artistic value.

The **Crypt.** The Crypt is situated below the Presbytery. It has a low ceiling and many columns which divide the space into several short, narrow naves or aisles. The altar, which is immediately below the main altar of the Basilica, was where the remains of St. Mark rested until recently when they were removed for fear of damage from flooding, and placed in the granite block which serves as the main altar of the Basilica. The **Marciano Museum and the Galleries**. The Museum and the exterior balconies and galleries of the Basilica are reached from the Narthex: the door on the right after the first five steps up into the Basilica having entered by the main door from the Square. The collection of the Museum is displayed in rooms immediately above the Narthex and includes sacred vestments, lace, tapestries, brocades and carpets. There are examples of both local and foreign craftsmanship, and the collection is both old and extremely valuable. In another two rooms examples of several different styles of mosaic work can be seen in pieces taken in past centuries from the walls of the Basilica. In a further larger room can be seen the Four Horses which until recently stood on the gallery of the main facade of the Basilica. The delicate state of the horses and the need to protect them from the elements has necessitated their removal from the gallery to this safer place. The galleries which run round three sides of the Basilica offer spectacular views which change with the shifting light and shadow of the Venetian day.

The Basin with Saint George seen from the roof of the Basilica

The Basin, night view ►

The Ducal Palace. Facade on the Piazzetta
St. Mark's Basin. Gondoliers

THE DUCAL PALACE

This palace fulfilled three functions: it was the
private residence of the Doge, the seat of
government and the court of justice of the
Serenissima Republic. Its various rooms were put to
different uses over the centuries, but in general it
would be true to say that on the first floor were sited
the offices, on the second, four large meeting rooms
for the members of some of the institutions of
government and the private apartment of the Doge,
and the third, great assembly halls. The original
rectangular Byzantine style Palace was begun in the
9th. century. It was defended by four towers, one at
each corner. Over the centuries, fire destroyed both
the interior decorations and the building itself. In the
14th. century the Palace was completely rebuilt,
starting on the side of the Paglia Bridge and
proceeding to the statue of Justice placed on the side
facing the Piazzetta. Later, work was continued and
by 1438 the Palace was complete right round to the
Porta della Carta. Meanwhile the Great Council Hall
had been inaugurated in 1419 and work begun on its
fresco decoration. These frescoes were however
destroyed by yet another fire. Around the end of the
15th. century Antonio Rizzo completed his
construction of the Foscari Arch and in 1498 also
finished the Staircase of the Giants. Attention then
turned to the wing of the Palace which gives onto
the canal at the side, and then to the completion of
the Courtyard of the Senators. Bartolomeo
Monopola designed and built the Clock facade in the
17th. century.

The Ducal Palace.
Porta della Carta

The Ducal Palace.
Foscari Arch

58

Facade. The exterior of the Palace, in Gothic style, seems almost to embody a reversal of the basic principles of architecture, with the lighter and more airy part of the structure - the porticoes and the loggia - at the bottom, and the heavier mass of the walls above. The columns of the portico are surmounted by thirty-eight finely carved capitals, the finest of which are to be seen at the corners of the building. They represent a drunken Noah with his sons by Matteo Raverti, situated at the corner near the Paglia Bridge, Adam and Eve by Bartolomeo Bon at the corner near the columns in the Piazzetta, and the Judgement of Solomon by the Lamberti and Nanni di Bartolo next to the Porta della Carta. The main entrance into the Palace is the doorway next to the Basilica called the Porta della Carta, built by Bartolomeo Bon. During the Republic this splendid example of flamboyant Gothic architecture with its marble statues, niches and pinnacles was all covered in gold. Two bronze wells of the 16th. century by Alfonso Alberghetti and Nicolò dei Conti embellish the inner courtyard. The Scala d'Oro - the Golden Staircase - which rises from the first floor loggia around the courtyard, serves to connect the main entrance and the Staircase of the Giants with the apartment of the Doge and the council halls on the upper floors. It was constructed to designs by Jacopo Sansovino and derives its name both from the official and ceremonial nature of its function and also from the richness of the decoration of its ceiling with its stuccowork, mosaics and bas-reliefs.

The Ducal Palace.
The courtyard seen from The Giants' Staircase

The Ducal Palace, corner facing the Piazzetta. Adam and Eve (sculpture)

*The Ducal Palace.
The Loggia
overlooking the Basin*

*The Ducal Palace.
Golden Staircase*

The **Doge's Apartment**. The private residential quarters of the Doge are situated on the second floor and are reached by climbing the stairs to the right after the first flight of the Golden Staircase. The rooms which make up the apartment are the Room of the Scarlatti, the Hall of the Shield, and then a series of interconnecting rooms called the Grimani Room, the Erizzo Room, the Priuli Room or the Room of the Stucchi and the Hall of the Philosophers. Then follow the three rooms which formed the truly private part of the Doge's apartment, and finally the Room of the Scuderi or Squires. The visitor receives a general impression of luxury from the ceiling decoration of finely sculpted wood covered in gold leaf and the fireplaces in Lombardesque style. There is also an extremely fine fresco of St. Christopher by Titian that can be seen from the staircase connecting the Hall of the Philosophers and the third floor. Noteworthy too are the paintings of Hieronymus Bosch, the Winged Lion by Carpaccio and, in the Room of the Squires, Venice and Neptune by Giambattista Tiepolo. The visitor's itinerary, which can vary when the rooms are occupied by art exhibitions, takes us up the second flight of the Golden Staircase to the third floor, where the rooms can be seen in the following order: the Square Drawing-room; the Room of the Four Doors; the Ante-chamber of the Hall of the Collegium; the Hall of the Collegium itself, and finally the Hall of the Senate. We are now entering rooms which are renowned for their works of art, their luxurious decoration and for the atmosphere they create.

In the **Square Drawing-room** the ceiling is a kind of huge frame for the central painting by Tintoretto of Doge Priuli with Justice, Peace and St. Jerome. The **Room of the Four Doors** was used as a waiting room and this function is reflected both in the doors, framed with precious marbles and also in the subjects of the great paintings on the walls and the frescoes on the ceiling. On the right, between the doors, a painting by Titian depicts Doge Antonio Grimani adoring Faith. The **Ante-chamber of the Collegium** and the Hall itself are linked like the pronaos and the naos of a Greek temple, but at the same time clearly reflect the different functions they were called upon to perform. In the Ante-chamber there are five masterpieces to admire, four of them by Jacopo Tintoretto: Mercury and the Three Graces, The Marriage of Bacchus and Ariadne, Pallas and Mars, and Vulcan's Forge; the fifth painting is The Rape of Europa by Paolo Veronese.

Hall of the Four Doors

The Ante-chamber of the Collegium. Jacopo Tintoretto, Pallas and Mars

The Ante-chamber of the Collegium. Jacopo Tintoretto, The Marriage of Bacchus and Ariadne

Hall of the Collegium, ceiling ►

The **Hall of the Collegium** is perhaps the most refined and most sumptuous room in the whole Palace. Here met the members of the inner council of state known as the Signoria or Consiglio Minore, made up of the Doge and his Councillors, the Sages, the head of the Council of Ten and the Grand Chancellor. Here too were received princes and heads of state and their ambassadors, and the most important problems of state were discussed. The central paintings of the ceiling - Neptune and Mars, Faith, Venice enthroned with Peace and Justice, and the smaller paintings of the Virtues - as well as The Battle of Lepanto above the Throne are all masterpieces by Paolo Veronese.

NVNQVAM
DERELIC
TA.

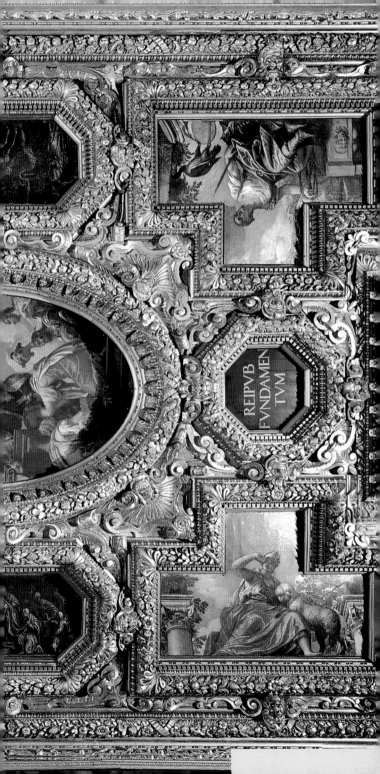

The **Hall of the Pregadi** (so-called because attendance at the meetings was by request of the Doge) or the Senate Hall is a richly decorated late 16th. century room. The two adjacent rooms were used as the Senate chapel. The **Hall of the Council of Ten** is part of an architectural complex which may well date from the original Palace. It was clearly visible as an independent entity before the restructuring which was carried out in the 16th. century and has its own staircases which lead from the ground floor right to the top of the building. Apart from the Hall of the Council of Ten, other aspects of the administration of the judiciary are seen to be reflected in the other rooms on this floor: the Hall of the Bussola which served as an ante-chamber to the Hall of the Council of Ten, the room of the Heads of the Council of Ten, the Room of the State Inquisitors and then the torture chambers and the prison cells known as the Piombi or Leads. Neither of the latter two areas is open to the public. The Hall of the Council of Ten is interesting both for its historical associations and also for two canvases by Paolo Veronese - Juno, Queen of the Gods, presents Venice with the Ducal Cap, and The Old and New States. In the Hall of the Bussola can be seen a Bocca di Leone - this is a hole hollowed out in the wall reached through the open mouth of a lion, the symbol of Venice, where citizens could place written accusations. The painting at the centre of the ceiling of the Room of the Three Heads of the Council of Ten is by Paolo Veronese and represents The Punishment of the Forger.

The **Room of the State Inquisitors** is small and lined with shelves. The ceiling was decorated by Jacopo Tintoretto with paintings symbolizing the Virtues and, in the centre, The Return of the Prodigal Son. The **Armoury**. The Armoury occupies some rooms of the Torresella, an ancient prison, and the room which, since the 16th. century contained the arms of the Council of Ten. The collection has recently been reorganized for display. The original nucleus of the collection - the arms of the Council of Ten - was subsequently enriched by bequests of noble families and gifts donated by visiting princes and fighting men. As a collection of weapons it is extremely rich and contains several specimens renowned for their fine workmanship. There is a suit of armour belonging to Henry IV, King of France, a Turkish pennant, captured at the Battle of Lepanto, a bronze colubrine by Alfonso Alberghetti, a grapeshot arquebus of the 17th. century and various swords, pikes, arquebuses, broadswords and muskets.

The Hall of the Pregadi, or Senate

The Ducal Palace, the Armoury. The Henry IV Room

The Ducal Palace, the Armoury. Gattamelata's equestrian armour

The **Hall of the Quarantia Civil Vecchia** and the Hall of the Old Armoury open off a corridor on the second floor. In the first room met a kind of Court of Appeal which dealt with both criminal and civil suits; on the walls of the second are displayed the remains of the frescoes which Guariento painted for the Hall of the Great Council between 1365 and 1367 - The Coronation of the Virgin. This part was recovered from the wall which now bears the great canvas of Jacopo Tintoretto. The **Hall of the Maggior Consiglio** or Great Council. The room is 54 metres long, 25 metres wide and 15.4 metres high. It is a completely open space, uninterrupted by columns or pillars and the window apertures which reach high up the walls and the ceiling and wall decorations and pictures give it a very special kind of atmosphere. This was where the Maggior Consiglio sat, the body whose privilege it was to nominate the Doge, the Senators, the Procurators as well as to debate laws, sanction peace and declare war. The present paintings were executed in the second half of the 16th. century and had as their themes the glorification of Venice (ceiling, central pictures), the most famous victories (ceiling, side pictures), and the three principal episodes in Venetian history, Doge Sebastiano Ziani acting as intermediary to achieve peace between Pope Alexander III and Frederick Barbarossa (right wall), the Fourth Crusade (left wall), and the victorious return from Chioggia of Doge Andrea Contarini after his defeat of the Genoese fleet (end wall). On the wall above the entrance is Tintoretto's Paradise. High up on the walls and below the ceiling can be seen idealized portraits of the first seventy-eight Doges of Venice. The **Hall of the Quarantia Civil Nuova**. This room was where civil cases against inhabitants of Venice's mainland territories were heard.

The Ducal Palace, Room of the Three Heads of the Council of Ten

The Ducal Palace, Great Council Hall

Hall of the Scrutinio. This room was the scene of the final act in the election of the Doge and the voting for other high offices of state. High up on the walls, just below the ceiling the portraits of the last forty-two Doges can be seen. Continuing the theme of the glorification of Venice and her sons, besides the Last Judgement by Jacopo Palma the Younger (entrance wall), the paintings on the ceiling and walls include: The Battle of Zara by Jacopo Tintoretto (right wall); The Battle of Lepanto by Andrea Vicentino (left wall, centre); The Battle of the Dardanelles by Pietro Liberi (right wall). On the end wall a triumphal arch in celebration of Francesco Morosini frames the exit door.

The Ducal Palace. Hall of the Scrutinio

The Bridge of Sighs and the Prisons. The visit to the Ducal Palace itself ends here, but it is worth retracing our steps to cross the Bridge of Sighs for a visit to the Prisons before we leave. First, we pass throught the Hall of the Quarantia Criminale and then through the Hall of the Magistrature. In the latter room can be seen the original marble statues of Adam and Eve which were once sited in niches on the Foscari Arch in front of the Staircase of the Giants but have now been replaced by bronze copies. The way now leads over the Bridge of Sighs, a covered passage over the canal between the Palace and the Prisons. The Bridge of Sighs became famous in the Romantic era, but in the time of the Republic its name was associated more with the idea of the punishments about to be suffered by those who crossed it. The New Prisons across the Rio del Palazzo were built by Antonio Contin in the

16th. century.

Bridge of Sighs

Matteo Raverti, Noah drunk and the Bridge of Sighs

SAINT GEORGE
GRAND CANAL

1-Saint George. 2-Grand Canal

SAINT GEORGE

In front of us opens Saint Mark's Basin with the Mint (Zecca) on the right, the Ducal Palace on the left, followed by the long and curved shore of the Riva degli Schiavoni leading as far as the island of Sant'Elena, which was at one time the site of a large number of shipyards. Facing us is Saint George, in ancient times called the Island of Cypresses for the cypress-trees that grew there. In 982 it was made over as a grant to Giovanni Morosini by the Republic, and he founded a Benedictine monastery there, which as a result of special privileges and bequests received from Emperors, Popes and Doges, in particular from Sebastiano Ziani (buried here in 1178), was thus continually enriched in such a way as to soon become a religious and cultural centre of European fame. The buildings which were raised here, were all destroyed in the earthquake of 1223 and reconstructed with the assistance of the Doge Pietro Ziani who died on this peaceful island in 1229.

Gondolas in the Basin

Accademia Gallery.
Francesco Guardi,
St. Mark's Basin and St. George

St. George, Laurel Cloister

Gondolas with St. George in the background ▶

From the first half of the 15th. cent. onwards work was to continue steadily until the early years of the 17th. cent. Cosimo, Lord of Florence, while exiled at Padua, visited Venice and lived on this island for a brief period. The architect Michelozzo Michelozzi, whom Cosimo had brought with him, constructed the Library, the first example in Venice of Renaissance architecture, which unfortunately was later pulled down. The Dormitory (known as the Manica Lunga or Long Sleeve) is a fascinating building, above all in the interior, with its cells in the two wings and a central corridor 128 metres long by Giovanni Buora. The Laurel Cloister, built on Giovanni Buora's plans, was finished by his son Andrea. On the other sides the guests' quarters and the residence of the Abbot were built. The Chapter House also forms part of the 16th. cent. complex of buildings. From 1559 onwards Palladio worked on the island. He built the Refectory between 1559 and 1563; the Church of Saint George with its square begun in 1579 and finished around 1610; the Cypress Cloister between 1579 and 1614. After the death of Palladio (1580) the buildings were completed by other architects. In the 17th. cent. the last constructions were executed by Longhena, notably the Grand Stairway in the first cloister (1641-1643), the Apartments of the Abbots overlooking Saint Mark's Basin and the Library (1641-1671).

Church of Saint George, interior

The Island of Saint George, aerial view

*A gondola
with Saint George
in the background*

GRAND CANAL

The Grand Canal is the most important of the city's canals and is unique amongst the main throughfares of the world. Already by 1495 the splendour and riches of the palaces which lined both banks of the canal were an object of wonder to the ambassador of Charles VIII, Philippe de Commines.

Grand Canal.
Aerial view of Rialto Bridge

Grand Canal. Aerial view

The Regatta. A gondola race in which the strongest oarsmen of the city and the entire estuary take part. A holiday, with a parade of gondolas and other boats before the main event, decorated with multicoloured fabrics and with the oarsmen dressed in traditional costume. And the spectators, who watch the celebrations from spacious barges, add a further touch of liveliness and noise to the proceedings.

*Regatta Day on the
Grand Canal*

Punta della Dogana. This was the place where goods arriving in Venice by sea were cleared of customs inspections and import taxes. In the early centuries of the city's existence this was the site of a battlemented tower which was part of the defensive strategy against pirates. The present tower, surmounted by a globe and statue of Fortune, was built by the architect Giuseppe Benoni in the 17th. century. **Basilica della Salute.** The construction of the church of S. Maria della Salute a masterpiece of Baroque art, was completed by Baldassare Longhena in the 17th. century. The renown of the basilica arises both from its wonderful site, dominating the entrance to the Grand Canal and also from the architect's skilful manipulation of volumes and spaces and the picturesque steps which rise out of the water up to the level of the church itself. The interior is based on a circular plan with the high altar immediately opposite the main entrance. A rich collection of paintings adorns the various altars and the Sacristy. Of particular interest are Luca Giordano's pictures on the three altars to the right, the Presentation, the Assumption and the Birth of the Virgin; on the third altar to the left can be seen a Pentecost by Titian and in the Sacristy St. Mark and Saints, Abraham's Sacrifice, David and Goliath and Cain and Abel all by Titian and the Marriage at Cana by Tintoretto.

Basilica della Salute

Venier dei Leoni Palace. Guggenheim Collection

Palazzo Dario

Abbey of San Gregorio. During the Middle Ages the Abbey was one of the important religious institutions of the city. The portal with a relief of the saint (14th. century) and the cloister both date from the time of the original building. **Palazzo Dario**. The palace was completed by Pietro Lombardo in the 15th. century. **Guggenheim Collection**. A private collection of modern works of painting and sculpture. **Palazzo Barbarigo**. Built in the 16th. century, it was decorated with mosaics in the 19th. century.

Palazzo Contarini-Fasan. A 15th. century Flamboyant Gothic palace in which the different proportions of the arches betray the influence of the new Lombardesque style. **Palazzo Corner della Cà Grande**. In this palace which Jacopo Sansovino built for the Corner family, the architect achieved artistic perfection in the classical lines of the facade. The impulse towards the decorative which is clear in the outlining of the stone-work and of the columns and spaces is firmly controlled by the architect's sense of balance. The entrance from the street is through a majestic portal into a courtyard where stands a statue of Apollo by Francesco Cabianca in the 17th. century. At present, the building is used as the offices of the Prefecture.

Palazzo Barbarigo

Palazzo Grassi

Palazzi Barbaro. The original parts of these palaces date from the 15th. century and reconstructional work from the 17th. century. As a result, they offer examples of Gothic, Renaissance and even Baroque style. **Accademia Bridge**. The bridge was built in the 19th. century. **Palazzetto Falier**. The palace was originally built in the 15th. century and when restoration work was carried out in subsequent centuries two wings were added. **Palazzo Grassi**. Commissioned by the Grassi family, the architect Giorgio Massari built this magnificent palace opposite Palazzo Rezzonico in the 18th. century. The rooms are ranged around an interior courtyard and the ones on the facade side give onto the water almost as if to welcome it. In fact this palace is perhaps the best example of that fusion of water and interior which is so distinctive of the architecture of Venice. A very significant indication of the customs of the 18th. century is the fresco on the wall of the main staircase, painted by Alessandro Longhi. **Palazzo Contarini dalle Figure**. The building dates from the 16th. century. **Palazzo Corner-Spinelli**. Built by Mauro Coducci over the end of the 15th. century and the beginning of the 16th. this palace is a remarkable example of decorative effects achieved through the arches of the windows, the balconies and, above all, the severe sense of balance which pervades the whole facade. **Palazzo Corner-Contarini dai Cavalli**. This palace in Flamboyant Gothic style dates from the 15th. century. Only the central balcony remains of the original elegant construction.

Palazzo Contarini dal Zaffo. One of the most beautiful buildings of the early Renaissance, this palace was constructed by Mauro Coducci around the end of the 15th. century. Still visible are the various decorative elements with which the architect adorned the facade.

**Accademia Bridge. Accademia Gallery.
Palazzo Mocenigo-Gambara.
Palazzo Contarini dagli Scrigni.
Palazzo Loredan dell'Ambasciatore.**

Palazzo Rezzonico. The building of this imposing 17th. century palace was supervised up to the 2nd. floor by Baldassare Longhena while the 3rd. floor was completed by Giorgio Massari. Entrance from the street is through a grandiose portal into the courtyard which occupies the central part of the ground floor almost all its length. Displayed in rooms throughout the palace are works of art and decorative articles and the palace is open to the public as a **Museum of Eighteenth Century Venice** (see page 118).

Palazzo Giustinian. A Gothic construction of the mid-15th. century. In the third section of the building which is now connected to Cà Foscari, Richard Wagner composed the second act of Tristan and Isolde (1858-1859).

Palazzo Foscari. A Gothic construction of the second half of the 15th. century, Cà Foscari was the residence of Doge Francesco Foscari who died here in 1457. The building is now the seat of the University of Venice. **Palazzo Balbi**. The building was designed by Alessandro Vittoria and was completed in the 16th. century. **Palazzo Pisani-Moretta**. A Gothic construction dating from the mid-15th. century. The great rooms of the palace acquired considerable fame over the centuries for the paintings which decorated them; works by Veronese, Giambattista Tiepolo and Giambattista Piazzetta. Only a few of the paintings now remain in their original places. **Palazzo Barbarigo della Terrazza. Palazzo Cappello-Layard. Palazzo Grimani**. An elegant Lombardesque construction of the 15th.-16th. centuries. Its fine proportions, the decorative whiteness of the marble, the admirable sculptures of the pillars all combine to create an effect of extremely refined taste. **Palazzo Bernardo**. A notable example of Gothic architecture of the mid-15th. century. **Palazzo Donà. Palazzo Coccina-Tiepolo-Papadopoli**. The palace was built by Giangiacomo dei Grigi around the mid-16th. century. It once contained important collections of paintings, coins and glass which are now for the most part dispersed amongst various museums. **Palazzo Businello. Palazzo dei Dieci Savi**. Only the smaller of the facades of this early 16th. century building is visible from the Grand Canal.

Palazzo Rezzonico

Palazzo Pisani - Moretta

Palazzo Grimani di San Luca. The masterpiece of the architect Michele Sanmicheli, Palazzo Grimani was completed in the first half of the 16th. century. Typical of Sanmicheli, whose work at Verona gave the architecture of that city a style all its own, are the architraves, the pillars and the columns which separate the deeply recessed arched windows. **Palazzo Corner-Martinengo. Palazzi Loredan-Farsetti.** These are two 13th. century Veneto-Byzantine buildings, radically transformed by restoration and additional upper-storeys. Handling of facade, distribution of ground-floor rooms and spacious garden at the rear of the premises are in conformity with the architectural canons of the Byzantine house-warehouse. **Palazzo Bembo**. Incorporated into the walls of this imposing Gothic edifice can be seen architectural and decorative elements of previous constructions on the site. **Palazzo Dolfin-Manin**. The classical facade of this palace was designed by Jacopo Sansovino in the 16th. century. It was the residence of the last Doge of Venice, Ludovico Manin, and has undergone many transformations over the centuries, the last being the establishment there of the offices of the Bank of Italy.

Grand Canal, Rialto Bridge

Grand Canal, Rialto Bridge, night view

Rialto Bridge. The area now known as Rialto, which once gave its name to the whole group of islands on which the city was built, was from the beginning the centre of the commercial activity of the lagoon dwellers. As early as the 12th. century the volume of people and goods needing to be transported from one bank of the Grand Canal to the other at this point made the construction of a bridge to replace the old ferry-boat system necessary. The wooden bridge with a drawbridge section was called the "quartarolo" after the coin which had to be paid as a toll to cross it. This construction was restored and rebuilt several times but by the 16th. century it was clear that it too was unable to carry the volume of traffic necessary so the government ordered a new bridge to be built of stone. The most famous of contemporary architects from Michelangelo to Palladio, from Sansovino to Scamozzi and Da Ponte all presented projects. The design eventually chosen, and that only in part, was the one entered by Andrea Da Ponte and in 1587 he began work on the new bridge with his nephew Antonio Contin. Work was completed in 1591 during the reign of the Doge Pasquale Cicogna. Situated on the single arch of the bridge are two rows of shops and three pedestrian passageways. As a work of art the Rialto Bridge has many critics but it is a functional work and still today provides the city with a symbol of its antiquity and exotic nature.

Palazzo dei Camerlenghi. This Lombardesque construction was built in the reign of Doge Andrea Gritti between 1525 and 1528, perhaps by the architect Guglielmo Bergamasco. The building offers a fine example of balance between architectural and decorative elements. It was the headquarters of the three Chamberlains whose responsibility it was to look after the financial affairs of the state of Venice.

Grand Canal, Rialto. Fishmarket

Grand Canal. Rialto. The market area

Fabbriche Nuove di Rialto. Fishmarket. Casa Favretto. Palazzo Corner della Regina. The present building, designed by the architect Domenico Rossi in the 18th. century, stands on the site of a former palace which was the birthplace of Caterina Cornaro, Queen of Cyprus.

Palazzo Corner della Regina

Palazzo Pesaro

Palazzo Pesaro. A remarkable example of Baroque style, the play of light and shadow on its majestic facade is heavily accentuated by the sharp division of its three floors. The construction is characterized by the consummate way in which the designer balanced the architectural masses and the decorative elements. The building is a masterpiece by Baldassare Longhena who died at the end of the 17th. century without completing the work. The third floor was finished by Antonio Gaspari in 1710. In the interior are displayed the collections of paintings and sculptures of the **Museum of Modern Art**. On show are works by the painters Teodoro Matteini, Francesco Hayez, Giacomo Favretto, Guglielmo Ciardi; and then Luigi Nono, Pietro Fragiacomo, Alessandro Milesi, Ettore Tito and the contemporary artists Guido Cadorin, Marco Novati and others. Also to be seen are works by Telemaco Signorini and Giovanni Fattori. The collection of sculpture includes examples of the work of Rodin and Antoine Bourdelle amongst other.

Fondaco dei Tedeschi. Completed by the architects Spavento and Abbondi in 1508, the building was used as the headquarters in Venice of merchants and traders of German nationality. The construction of the facade is characterized by the long portico at the centre of the base and two corner units which were once surmounted by towers. As soon as the construction was finished the artist Giorgione of Castelfranco set about painting his frescoes of imposing nudes between the windows but now time and salt air have practically destroyed them. **Campiello del Remer**. Here are visible the remains of Palazzo Lion-Morosini. **Cà da Mosto**. The building as it stands still retains many features of the original house-warehouse of the 13th. century: the portico at ground floor level, the rounded Byzantine arches on the first floor and the decorative elements set into the wall.

Cà da Mosto

Grand Canal. View of Cà d'Oro

Palazzo Michiel del Brusà. The present building takes its name from the fire which destroyed the Gothic style palace formerly on this site. **Palazzo Michiel dalle Colonne. Palazzo Foscari. Palazzo Sagredo. Cà d'Oro**. This palace is perhaps the most extraordinary example of Gothic architecture in Venice: the inventiveness of the decorative elements, the play of volumes and spaces, the lightening crown of lacy crenellations and above all the clear attempt to allow light and air to penetrate the wall of the facade. Gothic architecture, but interpreted and executed with oriental taste. Architects involved in the construction of the palace for Marin Contarini between 1421 and 1440 were Matteo Raverti and the Bon family. At the moment the whole building is being subjected to radical restoration work. Normally its rooms house the **art collection of Baron Giorgio Franchetti**. The collection contains paintings by Titian, Carpaccio, the Bellini family, portraits by Van Dyck, St. Sebastian by Mantegna and many "objets d'art". **Palazzo Gussoni-Grimani della Vida. Palazzo Barbarigo**. The facade of this 16th. century palace still shows traces of the frescoes painted by Camillo Ballini in the 16th. century. **Palazzo Erizzo**. This Gothic palace has undergone several restorations over the centuries, and since its completion in the 15th. century its ownership has passed through many hands.

Palazzo Foscarini-Giovanelli. Palazzo Tron. Palazzo Belloni-Battaglia. Baldassare Longhena designed and built this palace around the middle of the 17th. century, decorating the facade in the somewhat heavy style of the period. **Depositi del Megio**. A construction typical of the 15th. century with exposed brickwork, small marble-lintelled windows and lacy crenellations crowning the top. It was used as a warehouse for foodstuffs by the government and at present the premises are used as a school.

Depositi del Megio

Fondaco dei Turchi. Though the building has been subjected to radical restoration work, it is still possible to see the characteristic features of the house-warehouse of 13th. century Venice. The original building had, like the present building, a wide portico at ground floor level open from the canal to the inner courtyard and bounded by the two wings of the palace. Over the centuries the building underwent many modifications dictated by the various families through whose hands it has passed and it is now the **Museum of Natural History. Scalzi Bridge. Church of S. Simeon Piccolo. Papadopoli Gardens. Piazzale Roma.**

Fondaco dei Turchi

Palazzo Loredan-Vendramin-Calergi

Palazzo Marcello. Palazzo Loredan-Vendramin-Calergi. A good example of late-Renaissance style in Venice, this palace was built in the second half of the 15th. century. Designed by Mauro Coducci, it was completed by Lombardo in 1509, and offers the best example of the architectural taste of the period with its exquisite balance between the sections of the facade and the two-lighted mullioned windows. Many families have owned the palace over the years and it was here in 1883 that Richard Wagner died. **Palazzo Martinengo-Mandelli. Palazzo Corner Contarini. Palazzo Labia. Church of S. Geremia. Palazzo Flangini. Palazzo Calbo-Crotta. Railway Station.**

ACCADEMIA GALLERY
CAMPO SANTO STEFANO
CHURCH OF SAN MOISE'

1-Accademia Gallery. 2-Campo Santo Stefano. 3-Church of San Moisè

ACCADEMIA GALLERY

The Gallery possesses the most important collection of Venetian painting from its origins up to the 18th. century and is famous throughout the world for certain extremely rare and beautiful works and also for the high quality of the collection.

Room I. Here are displayed pictures of the 14th. century, by primitive masters. The various polyptychs and paintings of religious or symbolic subjects were the work of the artists who were fundamental to the establishment of a school of Venetian painting: Jacobello del Fiore, Paolo and Lorenzo Veneziano and Michele Giambono. In the paintings the influence of mosaics is clearly felt in the gold backgrounds which gradually give way to meadows, flowers, trees; the influence of Byzantine art in the elongated figure drawing and the wide-open staring eyes of the subjects; and the influence of Gothic style in the arrangement of the figures always grouped around a central point like the Virgin Mary or Christ and the Virgin Mary together.

Room II. The altar-pieces displayed in the second room take us on to the second half of the 15th. century and to the full flowering of the style of the Venetian School. Giovanni Bellini: Virgin Enthroned with Saints; Deposition. Vittore Carpaccio: Presentation at the Temple; The Ten Thousand Martyrs. Giambattista Cima da Conegliano: The Doubting of St. Thomas; the Madonna of the Orange Tree; Virgin and Saints. Marco Basaiti: The Prayer in the Garden; The Calling of the Sons of Zebedee. G.

Bellini offers an example of his gentle, thoughtful Madonnas and of the ideal setting in which his subjects pray without posing and suffer without melodrama.

Room IV. A group of paintings from the second half of the 15th. century which, though they derive from various different cultural backgrounds, all contributed in some way to the formation of a School of Venetian painting. From Padua, Andrea Mantegna: St. George. From Florence, Piero della Francesca: St. Jerome. From Ferrara, Cosmè Tura: Madonna and Child. From Holland, Hans Memling, Portrait of a Young Man.

Room V. Here hang two paintings by Giorgione of Castelfranco: The Tempest; The Old Woman; and a series of works by Giovanni Bellini including a Pietà and several treatments of the Madonna and Child theme. The visitor can see how Giambellino's Madonnas evolved away from the influence of Mantegna towards a perfection of form and content which he manages to synthesize in an idealized sweetness. It was without doubt Giorgione of Castelfranco who, in the first decade of the 16th. century, took the stylistic possibilities inherent in the Venetian School to their highest degree of perfection. The Tempest is a forerunner of what came to be known as tonal painting and shows how a genre scene might have been conceived at that time. A stream runs down through a landscape of trees and buildings. In the foreground on the right a young woman, semi-nude, is breast-feeding a child, and on the opposite bank a young man stands watching. Not far off a broken column can be seen. What the painter really seems to be trying to do is to penetrate the substance of the paint and make it ferment to give an almost tactile reality to Nature, to the whirlpools, a real depth to the water, lightning flashes in a wild sky still full of rain which has already fallen on the man who seems to be awakening as a result and on the woman whose hair is still damp.

Accademia Gallery. Giorgione, The Tempest

Room VI. Three of the paintings in this room are for different reasons very important. Paris Bordone: The Fisherman Bringing the Ring to the Doge; Bonifacio Pitati: Lazarus and the Rich Man; and Titian: John the Baptist.

Room X. The most important group of paintings in the Gallery's collection hangs here. Titian: Deposition; Paolo Veronese: The Feast in the House of Levi; Jacopo Tintoretto: Crucifixion; Portrait of the Procurator Soranzo and the eight canvases which depict the miracles of St. Mark, paintings which originally hung in the Scuola of St. Mark. The Deposition was Titian's last work, left unfinished at his death and completed by Jacopo Palma the Younger as noted in the Latin inscription on the painting. The cycle of paintings dedicated to St. Mark come from a crucial period in the development of Tintoretto's technique. In the picture entitled St. Mark frees the Slave of 1548 Tintoretto manages to move beyond the influence of Michelangelo and through his quality of light and his figure arrangements to achieve an artistic balance of the very highest level.

Room XI. Paolo Veronese: The Battle of Lepanto, The Marriage of St. Catherine, The Annunciation, The Crucifixion, St. Francis Receiving the Stigmata, St. Nicholas Arriving at Myra, Allegory of Venice. The painter's use of colour is so rich and luxurious that it is difficult for the viewer to participate in the tragedy of the Crucifixion. Some of the other paintings offered subjects which were closer to his nature both as man and as artist. Here the figures become almost superabundant and richly presented, though the composition is always identifiably classical in feeling. Jacopo Tintoretto: Cain and Abel, Adam and Eve, The Creation.

Room XI (second part). Bernardo Strozzi: Banquet at the House of Simon. Luca Giordano: Crucifixion of St. Peter. Giambattista Tiepolo: The Scourge of Serpents, Orantes, The Recovery of the True Cross.

Accademia Gallery. Vittore Carpaccio,
The Healing of the Demoniac

Accademia Gallery. Gentile Bellini,
Miracle of the Cross at San Lorenzo

Room XII. The pictures of Views and Ruins hung along the walls of the corridor lead us into the different world of the 18th. century, a world in which each of the painters has left us his different comment. In Giambattista Tiepolo the blue of the paintings of Veronese is transformed into a delicate pastel azure. The landscape artists Francesco Zuccarelli, Giuseppe Zais and Marco Ricci seem absorbed in Greek mythology and delight in painting carefully ordered Arcadian landscapes. Canaletto gives the buildings of the city a white patina which makes them look like stage scenery that a gust of wind might blow to the ground at any moment. In Guardi, Pietro Longhi and Rosalba Carriera the sense of miniature and detail attain their highest expression of the period.

Room XX. The paintings conserved in this room are important not only for their artistic value but also for the testimony they give of the appearance of Venice centuries ago. An excellent example of this is the Procession in Piazza San Marco by Gentile Bellini (1496) in which the painter offers a description of the Square, the Basilica, the Campanile and the buildings around all painted in the most revealing detail, even down to the exact shape of the chimneys and the layout of the paving-stones. Look too at Gentile Bellini: The Miracle of the Cross at San Lorenzo, and Vittore Carpaccio: The Healing of the Demoniac.

Room XXI. The landscapes, the water, the characters which inhabit the various scenes in the St. Ursula cycle of paintings exercise a special fascination. Vittore Carpaccio describes a fable-world, unreal and mysterious; even when painting detail he seems distracted by the curious, and when painting backgrounds he will place on the sea a galley with sails billowing in the wind immobile, as if it were enchanted or perhaps a toy ship waiting for a push to make it move forward.

*Accademia Gallery.
Vittore Carpaccio,
St. Ursula's Dream*

*Accademia Gallery.
Paolo Veronese.
The Feast in the
House of Levi*

Room XXIII. Gentile Bellini: The Blessed Lorenzo Giustinian; Giovanni Bellini: Triptych of the Nativity, Triptych of St. Sebastian; Bartolomeo Vivarini: Triptych of Conversano Bari; Carlo Crivelli: St. Jerome and St. Augustine.

Hostel of the School. Antonio Vivarini and Giovanni d'Alemagna: Triptych; Titian: The Presentation of the Virgin Mary at the Temple. This painting still occupies the place for which it was originally painted.

Church of San Vitale. The church was originally founded in the 11th. century but the present building dates only from the 18th. century. On the various altars can be seen the following paintings: Giambattista Piazzetta: Archangel Raphael and Saints; Vittore Carpaccio: St. Vidal and Saints and Four Saints before the Virgin; Sebastiano Ricci: The Virgin Conceived. **Campo Santo Stefano**. Palazzo Pisani is a gigantic construction and boasts two facades and a complex of courtyards and rooms large and small which clearly manifest the great wealth of the Pisani family. The building was completed in the 17th. century under the direction of the architect Girolamo Frigimelica. The refined stucco decorations of the interior are by Domenico Tiepolo, Jacopo Guarana and others. The building, now inevitably despoiled of its furniture and objets d'art, is used as the Conservatory and has taken the name of the Venetian composer Benedetto Marcello. Amongst the relics assembled at the Conservatory are the baton and music stand used by Richard Wagner during his last public performance in 1882. In the campo, a very busy square which is a much-favoured meeting-place for Venetians, can be seen Palazzo Morosini, the 17th. century residence of the Doge Francesco Morosini and also Palazzo Loredan. **Church of Santo Stefano**. Together with its monastery, the church was an important religious centre as is clear from the noble architecture of the building and the fine works of art it contains. It was completed in the 14th. century and offers numerous examples of Gothic stylistic features: the decoration around the main entrance, the vaulting of the nave in the form of a ship's keel, the columns and the capitals. Amongst the works of particular artistic and historical importance are the monumental tomb of Doge Francesco Morosini and, in the Sacristy, paintings by Gaspare Diziani: Flight into Egypt, Adoration of the Magi, Slaughter of the Innocents; by Jacopo Tintoretto: Last Supper, Washing of the Feet and Christ in the Garden; and by Paris Bordone: Baptism of Christ. Of considerable interest too are the wooden choir stalls behind the High Altar and the Cloister where traces remain of frescoes, some of which were painted by Giovanni Antonio de Sacchis, known as "il Pordenone". **Church of Santa Maria del Giglio**. The church has recently been restored. The facade was the work of the architect Giuseppe Sardi who supervised its construction in the 18th. century. Of particular interest are the baroque sculptures of the facade and in the interior. Jacopo Tintoretto: The Four Evangelists; and in the 17th. century Sacristy, the sculpture of the young St. John, attributed to Desiderio da Settignano; and Antonio Zanchi: Abraham dividing the World. **Church of San Moisè**. The most interesting aspect of the church is its facade by the architect Alessandro Tremignon, a picturesque example of Venetian baroque. The

campanile next to the church dates from the 13th. century.

Palazzo Contarini dal Bovolo, with its superb spiral staircase, is a Renaissance building constructed by G. Candi in 1499. The staircase, withdrawn, rises in the small campo and provides an unexpected sight as one turns the corner; this fact, besides the originality of its design, has contributed to its fame.

Campo Manin.
Palazzo Contarini
dal Bovolo

La Fenice Theatre

CHURCH OF SANTA MARIA FORMOSA
CHURCH OF SAINTS JOHN AND PAUL
CHURCH OF SAN ZACCARIA

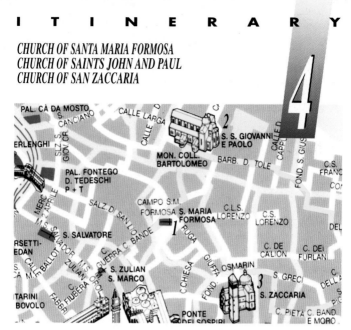

1-*Church of Santa Maria Formosa.* 2-*Church of Saints John and Paul.*
3-*Church of San Zaccaria*

Church of San Zulian. The church was the result of collaboration between the architects Jacopo Sansovino and Alessandro Vittoria in the 16th. century. The chief works of art to be seen are the bronze statue of Tommaso Rangone, the patron of the church, by Jacopo Sansovino, situated on the facade; and the paintings of the interior, including, by Paolo Veronese: The Dead Christ with Angels and Saints; by Antonio Zanchi: St. Julian on his way to Martyrdom and the Martyrdom of S. Julian; a Last Supper attributed to Paolo Veronese; Leonardo Corona: The Gift of Manna; Boccaccio Boccaccino: The Virgin Enthroned and Four Saints. **Church of Santa Maria della Fava**. The church was built by Antonio Gaspari and Giorgio Massari in the 18th. century. Apart from the interesting architecture, the following paintings are of note: Giambattista Tiepolo: St. Anne and Joachim with the Virgin Mary; Giambattista Piazzetta: St. Philip Neri in prayer before the Virgin. **Church of San Lio**. The original church on this site dates from very early times but the present building was constructed in the 17th. century. Worthy of special attention are James the Apostle by Titian and the Gussoni Chapel by the workshop of Pietro and Tullio Lombardo. **Church of Santa Maria Formosa**. The present church was completed from the designs of Mauro Coducci in 1492. The serene balance of volumes and space in the interior represents one of this architect's most successful solutions. The church is very compact and offers three facades to the square into which it seems to be projecting itself, a feature which emphasises the closeness of this particular church to popular traditions. Of special note are: Bartolomeo Vivarini: Madonna della Misericordia and Scenes from the Life of the Virgin; Jacopo Palma the Elder: Saint Barbara and Saints.

Campo Santa Maria Formosa, Rio del Paradiso

Querini-Stampalia Gallery. This Renaissance palace and the collection of paintings and books it contained was donated to the city of Venice by Count Giovanni Querini-Stampalia in 1868. The art gallery is situated on the second floor and contains works by Venetian painters of the 14th. 15th. and 16th. centuries and by other artists of the 17th. and 18th. centuries. Amongst the most important are: Gabriele Bella: Scenes of Public Life in Venice; Donato and Caterino: The Coronation of the Virgin; Lorenzo di Credi: Adoration of the Child; Giovanni Bellini: Presentation in the Temple; Jacopo Palma the Elder: Madonna and Saints; Vincenzo Catena: Judith with the Head of Holofernes; Pietro Longhi: The Sagredo Family and other works including Duck Hunt in the Lagoon; Giambattista Tiepolo: Portrait of a Procurator.

Querini Stampalia Picture Gallery.
P. Longhi, Duck Hunt

Church of Santa Maria dei Miracoli. Built between 1481 and 1489 by Pietro Lombardo and his masons the church is of compact dimensions and seems to reach upwards rather than outwards. The interior and exterior walls are faced with precious marbles set in the shape of crosses and other motifs presenting an aspect of exquisite, rather oriental taste.

Church of Saints John and Paul (Ss. Giovanni e Paolo). The church is only part of the complex of buildings which in past centuries functioned as the religious centre of the Dominican Friars. The other buildings in fact still stand but now the monastery houses the main hospital of the city, and the adjacent Scuola of St. Mark is used for meeting and conference rooms, and as a chemist's, leaving only the church to pursue its original spiritual purpose. The church itself took two centuries to build, between the 13th. and 15th. centuries, and offers excellent examples of Gothic style in the ogival arched windows, the cross-vault and iron tie-beams. The facade bears some traces of Renaissance architecture, particularly in the main doorway. In the interior, two aisles flank the main nave and lead to south-facing apsidal chapels which light the whole church. The church is particularly rich in monumental tombs and several Doges are buried here. Amongst works of art of special interest are: Giovanni Bellini: St. Vincent Ferrer and Saints (second altar on the right); Giambattista Piazzetta: The Glory of St. Dominic (Chapel of the Sacrament-ceiling); Alvise Vivarini : Christ carrying the Cross (right transept); Paolo Veronese: The Annunciation, The Assumption, The Adoration of the Shepherds; Bartolomeo Vivarini: Saints (junction of left transept and nave). Works of sculpture are particularly numerous and almost cover the walls of the nave and apse. Pietro Lombardo: Monument to Doge Pietro Mocenigo (just inside the main door on the left); Delle Masegne (attr.): Monument to Doge Michele Morosini (right wall of the Presbytery); Giovanni Girolamo Grapiglia: Monument to Doge Leonardo Loredan (right wall of the Presbytery); Pietro and Tullio Lombardo: Monument to Doge Andrea Vendramin (left wall of the Presbytery); Paolo di Jacobello delle Masegne: Funeral Urn of Jacopo dei Cavalli (second apsidal chapel on the left); Lorenzo Bregno (attr.): Monument to Leonardo da Prato (left transept); Pietro Lombardo: Monument to Doge Pasquale Malipiero (left transept, past the door to the Sacristy); Pietro di Nicolò Lamberti (known as "il Pela") and Giovanni di Martino da Fiesole: Monument to Tommaso Mocenigo - (1423) - (left transept). Note also the 15th. century stained glass window in the right transept.

Campo Ss. Giovanni e Paolo. Andrea Verrocchio, Monument to Bartolomeo Colleoni

Monument to Bartolomeo Colleoni. When armed forces of the Repubblica Serenissima occupied Milan, they set Bartolomeo Colleoni free from the prison where he was incarcerated, and from that moment he offered his services to the Government of Venice. He continued to fight at the head of his mercenary forces until his death in his castle at Malpaga in 1475, and in his will left the sum of one hundred thousand ducats to the Republic on condition that a monumental statue be erected in his memory in St. Mark's Square. The government immediately commissioned Andrea Verrocchio, one of the most famous Florentine sculptors of the day, to execute the statue, but when it was completed the authorities modified the terms of the will, for no-one had ever been granted the honour of a statue in St. Mark's Square, and had it placed in front of the School of St. Mark in Campo Santi Giovanni e Paolo. The equestrian monument composed of four elements - the figure of Bartolomeo Colleoni, his helmet, his spurs and the horse - is a masterpiece of sculpture though it might be accused of somewhat exaggerating the heroic nature of the pose. The pedestal was erected by Alessandro Leopardi.

Scuola of St. Mark. The Scuola or Confraternity of St. Mark was one of the six great institutions of its kind in the city. They were charitable foundations and their headquarters, like this one dedicated to St. Mark, were real artistic centres. The building of the Scuola was entrusted to Pietro Lombardo who worked in collaboration with his sons Tullio and Antonio and also with the architect Giovanni di Antonio Buora. Later architects whose work is visible were Mauro Coducci (the top part of the facade) and Jacopo Sansovino who built the facade which faces the canal at the side. Note the remarkable relief sculptures on the facade, the columns in the entrance hall, the great staircase leading to the floor above and on the upper floor itself the chapel and the hostel of the Scuola with its carved and coffered ceilings. This was the Scuola where Jacopo Tintoretto painted the famous canvases which now hang in the Accademia Gallery in Venice and the Brera Gallery in Milan. **Arsenal Museum**. The Museum's collection is displayed in several rooms with access from Campo San Biagio and comprises models of various galleys, the remains of the Bucentaur, the ceremonial barge of the Doge, and other ancient naval vessels and weaponry. The Arsenal itself is a vast area of land, partly covered where, in the time of the Serenissima Republic, galleys were built and equipped for state use. The might of Venice depended on the output of the Arsenal and in fact this declined from the era of Venice's greatest power in the 12th. century when a galley a day was turned out and work was provided for 16.000 men. The Arsenal originated when, in the 12th. century, the government concentrated the activities of all the various small boatyards of the city in this one place, and from that time the area gradually grew to its present size. The Arsenal is still surrounded by crenellated walls which open to allow access by canals and the great ceremonial entrance with the marble lions which Doge Francesco Morosini had brought from Athens in the 17th. century. The entrance is the first example of Renaissance architecture in Venice and was completed in 1460. **Church of San Francesco della Vigna**. The church itself is a Renaissance construction, built by Jacopo Sansovino and the facade was completed later (1568-1572) by Andrea Palladio. Several interesting works can be seen in the church: Paolo Veronese (attr.): Resurrection of Christ (fourth chapel, right aisle); Antonio da Negroponte: Virgin Enthroned and Child; the cycle of sculptures in the side chapel to the left of the High Altar; Giovanni Bellini: Virgin and Child with Saints (Chapel of the Conception).

*Scuola of San Giorgio degli Schiavoni.
Vittore Carpaccio, St. Augustine in his Study*

The Grifalconi house at SS. Giovanni e Paolo

Scuola of San Giorgio degli Schiavoni. The Scuola or Confraternity of St. George is famous for the cycle of paintings by Vittore Carpaccio which decorate its walls. The pictures narrate stories from the lives of the three Patron Saints of the people of Dalmatia, St. George, St. Trifone and St. Jerome. The most famous of the works are St. George Killing the Dragon and St. Augustine in his study. This latter painting is interesting also as a testimony of how a study of a learned person of the time looked.

Church of San Giovanni in Bragora. Though the present building dates from the 15th. century, on this site previously stood one of the oldest churches in the city. To be seen inside are several works of art including paintings by Cima da Conegliano, Alvise Vivarini and Bartolomeo Vivarini. **Church of Santa Maria della Pietà**. The work of the architect Giorgio Massari, this 18th. century church has recently been restored. **Church of San Zaccaria**. The first religious buildings on this site were built in the 9th. century and the complex gradually grew in importance and wealth to include not only the church but also a monastery and its cloister. The present church building dates from the 15th. century, its interior is the work of Antonio Gambello and the facade is by Mauro Coducci. The religious centre always had close links with the government of the city through the noble families which were its patrons and whose members often retired there: in fact, the Doge paid an official visit to the church once a year. The church shows signs of buildings of various different eras: in the apse, the remains of the flooring of the original church; and the adjacent bell-tower is of the 12th. century. Amongst the decorations inside the church, the following are of particular interest: Giovanni Bellini: The Virgin Enthroned with Saints (first altar on the left); Bernardo Strozzi: Tobias and his Father (above the door to the Chapel of St. Athanasius); Andrea del Castagno: Frescoes (Chapel of St. Tarasius, 1442); Stefano di S. Agnese: Polyptych (Chapel of St. Tarasius); Giovanni and Antonio da Murano: Polyptych of St. Sabina and Christ (Chapel of St. Tarasius, 1443); Jacopo Tintoretto: The Birth of John the Baptist (Chapel of St. Athanasius); Antonio Van Dyck (attr.) Crucifixion.

Riva degli Schiavoni. Church of Santa Maria della Pietà

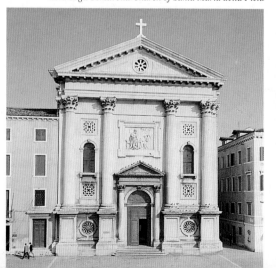

Riva degli Schiavoni.
Church of Santa Maria
della Pietà, interior

Church of San Zaccaria

CHURCH OF MADONNA DELL'ORTO
GHETTO
CHURCH OF SAN SALVADOR

1-Church of Madonna dell'Orto. 2-Ghetto. 3-Church of San Salvador

Church of Santi Apostoli. Of particular interest in the interior is the 15th. century Corner Chapel which is reputed to be the work of the architect Mauro Coducci. On the Chapel Altar can also be seen a painting by Giambattista Tiepolo: Communion of St. Lucy. **Church of the Jesuits** or of Santa Maria Assunta. A typical example of churches dedicated to the order of Jesuits: rich marble decorations, luxurious altars and a general sense of grandeur and opulence. Titian: The Martyrdom of St. Lawrence (first altar on the left). **Church of Madonna dell'Orto**. A Gothic building of the 15th. century with statues on the facade by Delle Masegne; the interior has undergone restorations which have profoundly changed the Gothic feeling of the architecture. In the interior are to be seen several fine works of art, especially by Jacopo Tintoretto who is buried here. Giambattista Cima da Conegliano: St. John the Baptist and Saints (first altar on the left); Jacopo Tintoretto: Presentation of Mary in the Temple (above the door into the Chapel of S. Mauro); Jacopo Tintoretto: The Hebrews worshipping the Golden Calf (left wall of Presbytery); Jacopo Tintoretto: The Last Judgement (right wall of Presbytery); Giovanni Antonio de Sacchis, known as "Pordenone": San Lorenzo Giustiniani and Saints (apsidal chapel on the left); Jacopo Tintoretto: St. Agnes brings the child of the Roman Prefect back to life (4th. Chapel - the Contarini Chapel); Giovanni Bellini: Madonna and Child (first chapel on left). **Church of Sant'Alvise**. Inside the church are three canvases by Giambattista Tiepolo: The Flagellation; The Crowning with Thorns; The Ascent to Calvary.

Church of Madonna dell'Orto

The Ghetto, segregating Jews from the remainder of the population, was set up in 1516. German Jewish migration was followed by that of Italian, Levantine and Spanish Jews, among the latter, those forcibly converted to Christianity. In 1797 the Ghetto gates were thrown open and since that time the Jewish community has taken part in city life alongside the rest of its citizenry. During the centuries of segregation, the Ghetto formed a tiny state separate by reason of religious belief, tradition and education. The Ghetto is laid out in three districts: Ghetto Vecchio (1541), Ghetto Nuovo (1516), Ghetto Nuovissimo (1663). The synagogues comprise: Scola Spagnola (Arch. Baldassare Longhena; 16th. century), Scola Levantina (1538), Scola Italiana (1575), Scola Canton (1531-32), Scola Grande Tedesca (1529). **The Museum of Jewish Art** houses traditional objects of the Jewish faith. A visit to the synagogues and the museum is of interest to all creeds for the light it throws on the culture of a community that made a precise contribution to Venetian life.

Church of S. Marziale. Several paintings by Sebastiano Ricci can be seen: The Eternal Father in Glory; The Glory of S. Marziale; The Arrival of the Image of the Virgin; the Image of the Virgin in a Tree-Trunk. **Church of Mary, the Mother of God** (S. Maria Mater Domini). The church gives onto a delightful campo which is remarkable for the variety of different styles to be seen in the buildings around its edge. Inside the church can be seen the masterpiece of Vincenzo Catena: The Martyrdom of Saint Christine. **Church of San Cassiano**. The church houses three paintings by Jacopo Tintoretto: The Descent into Limbo; The Crucifixion; and The Resurrection of Christ with Saints. **Church of S. Giacomo di Rialto**. The date generally considered to mark the birth of Venice is 451, the year in which refugees from the mainland first erected a chapel on this spot. The present church forms part of the complex known as the Rialto, the area of the market which was for several centuries the commercial centre of the Mediterranean. **Church of San Bartolomeo**. Three paintings by Sebastiano Luciani, known as "del Piombo", hang in this church: paintings of Saints Ludovico, Sinibaldo, Sebastiano and Bartolomeo. **Church of San Giovanni Grisostomo**. This is one of the religious buildings of Mauro Coducci and was constructed between 1497 and 1504. Several remarkable works of art are to be seen there: Giovanni Bellini: St. Jerome, St. Christopher and St. Augustine (first altar on the right); Sebastiano Luciani, know as "del Piombo": St. John Chrysostom and Saint John the Baptist, St. Liberale, St. Mary Magdalen, St. Agnes and St. Catherine (chapel to the right of the main altar); Tullio Lombardo: marble altar-piece with the Coronation of the Virgin with Apostles (chapel to the left of the main altar).

Cannaregio. Campo di Ghetto Nuovo

Church of San Salvador, interior

Church of San Salvador. As early as the 7th.
century this site was occupied by a religious
building, though the present one dates only from the
16th. century. The architects Tullio Lombardo,
Giorgio Spavento and Jacopo Sansovino all
contributed to the building of it. The facade was
completed to plans by Giuseppe Sardi in the 17th.
century. Many interesting works of sculpture and
painting adorn the interior. Jacopo Sansovino:
Monument to Doge Francesco Venier (second altar
on the right); Titian: The Annunciation (third altar
on the right); Bernardino Contino: Monument to
Caterina Cornaro, Queen of Cyprus (end wall in the
right transept); the very elegant Sacristy; Guglielmo
dei Grigi: the High Altar; Titian: Transfiguration
(on the High Altar); Giovanni Bellini: Supper at
Emmaus (apsidal chapel on the left); Bernardino
Contino: Funeral monument to three Cardinals of
the Cornaro family (left transept).

PALAZZO REZZONICO
CHURCH OF S. MARIA GLORIOSA DEI FRARI
SCUOLA GRANDE OF SAN ROCCO

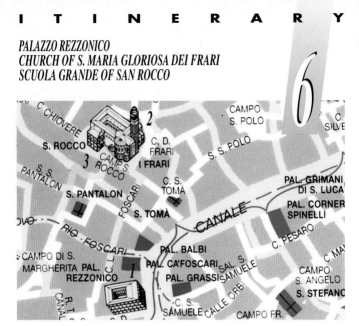

1-Palazzo Rezzonico. 2-Church of S. Maria Gloriosa dei Frari.
3-Scuola Grande of San Rocco

Church of San Giobbe. The church was designed and built by Pietro
Lombardo. **Church of St. Mary of Nazareth** or degli Scalzi. Baldassare
Longhena was the architect of the interior of the church while the facade
was designed by Giuseppe Sardi. During the First World War the interior
suffered irremediable damage from bombardments and the remains of the
frescoes which were salvaged from the ruins can now be seen in the
Accademia Gallery. The frescoes were executed by Giambattista Tiepolo in
collaboration with Gerolamo Mengozzi Colonna. Still visible in the church
itself are: Giambattista Tiepolo: St. Theresa in Glory (right aisle, first
chapel); Giovanni Marchiori: Statues of Sibyls (presbytery walls);
Giambattista Tiepolo: Christ in the Garden (vault of the third chapel on the
left). A detail of historical interest is that Ludovico Manin, the last Doge of
Venice, was buried in the second chapel on the left, the Manin Chapel.
Church of San Nicolò da Tolentino. The interior of this church is by
Vincenzo Scamozzi and the facade by Andrea Tirali. Of interest are the
following works: Bonifazio dei Pitati: The Beheading of John the Baptist,
The Feast in the House of Herod (the third chapel on the right, the Soranzo
Chapel); Luca Giordano: Annunciation (presbytery); Giovanni Lys: St.
Jerome (presbytery, left wall); Bernardo Strozzi: The Charity of St.
Lawrence (outside wall of the third chapel on the left).

Bridge and Church of the Scalzi

Grand Canal at San Simeon Piccolo, night view

Church of the Carmini. The church formed part of the monastery of the Carmelite friars. Amongst the works of art which adorn the interior are: Giambattista Cima da Conegliano: Nativity Scene with St. Helen, St. Catherine, the Guardian Angel and Tobias (right aisle, second altar); Bertoldo di Giovanni or Francesco di Giorgio Martini (attr.): Deposition with portraits of Federico da Montefeltro, his wife Battista Sforza and their son Guidobaldo (apsidal chapel on the right); Lorenzo Lotto: St. Nicholas in Glory with St. Lucy and John the Baptist, St. George killing the Dragon (right aisle). **Scuola of Santa Maria del Carmine**. Several important works are to be seen here: the masterpiece of Giambattista Tiepolo: The Virgin in Glory, with Virtues and Angels, offering the scapular to the Blessed Simon Stock (ceiling); Giambattista Piazzetta: Judith and Holofernes. **Palazzo Rezzonico, Museum of 18th. century Venice**. The rooms of the palace are decorated with paintings, frescoes, statues and collections of various sorts such as a puppet show complete with its puppets, robes and garments of noble families and their servants, pharmacy and a gondola all of 18th. century Venice. Amongst the most important works of art in the collection are: Giambattista Tiepolo: Nuptial Allegory (ceiling fresco, first floor); Rosalba Carriera: a series of pastels (Pastels Room, first floor); Jacopo Giacomo Guarana: Allegory of Virtue (Tapestry Room, first floor); Giambattista Tiepolo: Allegory of Merit between Nobility and Virtue (Throne Room, first floor); Giambattista Tiepolo: Strength and Wisdom (Tiepolo Room, first floor); Giambattista Piazzetta: The Death of Darius (second floor); Giovanni Lys: Judith and Holofernes (second floor); Pietro Longhi: a series of paintings depicting typical scenes in Venetian life (Longhi Room); Francesco and Antonio Guardi: The Ridotto and The Nuns' Parlour (rooms of the same name); Giandomenico Tiepolo: frescoes from the Villa Zianigo (second floor). The third floor contains the collection of costumes, the pharmacy and other exhibits.

Palazzo Rezzonico.
The Ballroom

Carnival. The carnival is a centuries-old tradition in Venice, which reached its maximum splendour in the 18th. century. At that time, the festival lasted for several months - from Christmas to Shrove Tuesday - and the masked inhabitants of the city and foreigners, both men and women, allowed themselves certain liberties that were forbidden during the rest of the year. The Carnival was restored to life some years ago and once again attracts locals and outsiders, eager to set aside the strict rules of behaviour laid down in everyday life. *119*

Church of Santa Maria Gloriosa dei Frari. The church is part of the complex of religious buildings occupied by the Franciscan friars and which included cloisters, cells and Chapter House. The church and the bell-tower date from the 14th. century and offer perhaps the best example of ogival style in Venice. The church is in the form of an Egyptian cross and its nave is flanked by two aisles. The Choir for the Friars still stands in its original position in the centre of the church. Many world-famous works of art can be seen, including, in the right and left aisles respectively, the funeral monument to Titian and that of the sculptor Antonio Canova; Giovanni

◄ *Frari Church*

Rosso Fiorentino: funeral monument to the Blessed Pacifico (right transept); Lorenzo Bregno: Monument to Benedetto Pesaro (over the door of the right transept); Giovanni Bellini: Virgin and Child with cherub musicians and four Saints (altar of the Pesaro Chapel in the Sacristy). This triptych is one of the finest masterpieces of all time and its three sections reach a perfect fusion of form and content: the pensive serenity of the Virgin and the seriousness of the Saints. From the Chapter House windows and the doorway can be seen one of the cloisters of the monastery. Jacopo della Quercia (attr.): Monument to Paolo Savelli (next to the sacristy door in the right transept); Bartolomeo Vivarini: Madonna with Cherubs and Saints (the third of the apsidal chapels - the Cà Bernardo Chapel); Donatello: painted wooden statue of St. John the Baptist (first chapel on the right, the Fiorentini altar); Titian: The Assumption (High Altar) - one of the artist's finest works. Antonio and Paolo Bregno: Monument to Doge Francesco Foscari (right wall of the presbytery); Antonio Rizzo: Monument to Doge Nicolò Tron (left wall of presbytery); Alvise Vivarini and Marco Basaiti: St. Ambrose enthroned between Saints and Angel Musicians (third apsidal chapel on the left); Jacopo Sansovino: statue of St. John the Baptist (Corner Chapel, baptismal font); Bartolomeo Vivarini: St. Mark and Saints (Corner Chapel, altar); Titian: Madonna and Child with Saints, known as the Cà Pesaro Madonna (left aisle, Pesaro Altar); Baldassare Longhena (attr.): Monument to Doge Giovanni Pesaro. The Friars' Choir stands in the place it has occupied since it was constructed in the 15th. century. The carved stalls are the work of Marco Cozzi (1468) and the seven marble pieces were produced under the supervision of the Bon family and Pietro Lombardo.

Frari Church.
Titian, The Assumption

Frari Church.
Cloisters

Campo San Rocco

Scuola Grande of San Rocco. Of the greatest cultural interest both for the quality of the building itself and for the masterpieces of art that it contains. Work was begun on the building in 1515 and was continued by Antonio Abbondi, known as "lo Scarpagnino", and later by Giangiacomo dei Grigi who finished it in 1560. As an example of Renaissance architecture in Venice the building is interesting for its layout, the facade, the double staircase which leads from the ground floor to the first. The whole feeling of the place gives an idea of elegance and luxury. Apart from the interest of the building itself, the Scuola Grande of San Rocco is famous throughout the world for the important cycle of paintings by Jacopo Tintoretto which he executed between 1564 and 1588.

The cycle of paintings on the ceilings and walls falls into two groups; subjects drawn for the stories of the New Testament on the ground floor and the walls of the first floor while Old Testament subjects appear on the ceilings of the first floor. Ground floor walls: Annunciation, Adoration of the Magi, Flight into Egypt, Slaughter of the Innocents, St. Mary Magdalene, St. Mary of Egypt, Circumcision, Assumption. The quality of light is the aspect which dominates these paintings and lends them an air of unreality. Walls, first floor: St. Rock, St. Sebastian, Nativity, Baptism, Resurrection, Prayer in the Garden, Raising of Lazarus, Ascension, Pool at Bethesda, Temptations of Christ, and a Self-portrait of the Artist: Ceiling: Moses causes water to run from the rock, Adam and Eve, God appears to Moses, The Crossing of the Red Sea, Jonah escapes from the belly of the Whale, The Miracle of the Bronze Serpent, Vision of the Prophet Ezekiel, Resurrection, Jacob's Ladder, Sacrifice of Isaac, The Miracle of the Manna, An Angel feeds the starving Elias in the Wilderness, Elias distributes bread to the multitude, The Feast of the Passover. Beside the altar can be seen: Titian: Annunciation; Jacopo Tintoretto: Visitation; Giambattista Tiepolo: Abraham and Angels and Hagar Abandoned. The various wood carvings in the Presbytery were executed by Giovanni Marchiori while Francesco Pianta the Younger completed the wooden figures set into the wall of the large hall. The hostel room too contains further masterpieces: in the ceiling, St. Rock in Glory, and on the walls, Christ before Pilate and the superb Crucifixion. This room also contains two famous paintings by Titian; Christ Carrying the Cross and The Dead Christ.

Querini-Stampalia Gallery.
G. Bella, the visit of a Doge at San Rocco

CHURCH OF THE GESUATI
CHURCH OF SAN SEBASTIANO
THE GIUDECCA

1-Church of the Gesuati. 2-Church of San Sebastiano. 3-The Giudecca

Church of the Gesuati. The work of the architect Giorgio Massari, the church contains the following works of special interest: Giambattista Tiepolo: The Institution of the Rosary; St. Dominic in Glory; St. Dominic on his Knees (ceiling); Virgin Enthroned with Saints (first altar on the right).
Church of San Sebastiano. The architect Antonio Abbondi, known as "lo Scarpagnino" was responsible for the building of the church itself, the facade and the bell-tower around the middle of the 16th. century. Of the utmost interest to the student of Venetian art are the paintings by Paolo Veronese who was also buried here. Apart from the paintings in the Sacristy, executed in 1555, other works of note are Esther summoned before King Ahasuerus, Esther Crowned by King Ahasuerus, Mordecai, the Uncle of Esther, carried in Triumph (the central panels of the ceiling); The Virgin and Child in Glory (altar-piece on the High Altar). **The Giudecca.** The islands of the Giudecca or Spinalunga gained their name perhaps because it was there that the first colony of Jews was established. These days passenger and cargo ships pass the Giudecca as they make their way along the Giudecca Canal towards the wharves and landing stages of the docks. Over the centuries the Giudecca has undergone several changes: in the 16th. century it was a retreat for noble families who had villas there surrounded by fine, spacious gardens. In the 16th. century Andrea Palladio built there the **Church of the Redentore** (Christ the Redeemer), perhaps the most remarkable of all the architect's works with its perfect marriage of spectacular site to classical design.

ESTUARY AND LITTORALS
TORCELLO
BURANO
MURANO   THE LIDO

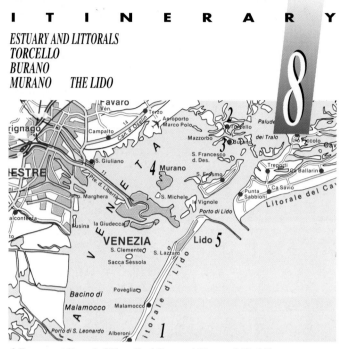

1-Estuary and Littorals. 2-Torcello. 3-Burano. 4-Murano. 5-The Lido

The visitor to Venice should not fail to take a trip around the islands of the lagoon and to the fishing villages of the islands which stand between the lagoon and the Adriatic. The unique landscape of the area is dominated by water, the element from which sea-gull covered islands rise, the element which catches the brilliant reflections of the brightly painted fishermen's cottages. **Torcello.** The name of the island probably derives from "Turricellum" and dates back to the times of the first barbarian invasions of the Veneto when refugees from the town of Altino nearby on the mainland came to settle here. It soon became a commercial centre of some importance and as a result permanent and significant buildings began to appear. The island continued to develop and the few buildings which have survived into our own times testify to the high level of civilisation that its inhabitants achieved.

Torcello, a Canal

Torcello. Piazzetta and Church of Santa Fosca

The island civilisation went into its period of decline when it became necessary to move to the more secure site of Rialto. The buildings they left behind date from the times of the Lombard invasions: the remains of the baptistry and the foundations of the Cathedral which was dedicated to Santa Maria Assunta. The mosaics of the interior of the Cathedral are remarkably beautiful: the Virgin, Mother of God (on the apse vault; 13th. century); the Lamb of God (ceiling of the lateral chapel on the right; 12th. century); Last Judgement (wall above the main entrance, 12th.-13th. centuries). The extremely elegant church nearby is dedicated to Santa Fosca and dates from the 11th.-12th. centuries.

Torcello, Cathedral.
Last Judgement (mosaic)

Torcello, Cathedral and Belltower

Burano
Burano, Varicoloured Houses
Lagoon fishermen

Burano. The ideal way to rest for a moment from the pilgrimage to works of art is to take a stroll alone around the island of Burano or the nearby S. Francesco del Deserto. The unique atmosphere of Burano arises from the unity of the place, the intimate connection between the inhabitants and the lagoon, the brightly coloured one-storey houses with their narrow entrances and the waters of the canals which flow past just outside. Between the inhabitants of the lagoon and the waters of the lagoon there has been for centuries a kind of common cause, a dialogue which will end only when one or the other breaks the treaty sanctioned by countless of the present generation's forefathers. The atmosphere of the island of **San Francesco del Deserto** is similar to that of Burano except that here the inhabitants are and always were friars of the Franciscan order. Their little monastery has its cloister, a church and all are set among cypress trees. But here too water is the element which dominates, and lends the colours and the air an almost tangible intensity.

Murano. This complex of islands stands between Burano and Venice and is known throughout the world for the particular quality of the glass which has been produced here for centuries - Murano glass. In the 16th. century many nobles had palaces with fine gardens built here and also obtained from the government of Venice special laws and privileges granted because of the important place glass production and export held in the economy of the city. As well as a visit to a glass factory, two churches and the Glass Museum are worth stopping to see. **Church of St. Peter Martyr**. Amongst the works to be seen in its interior are: Giovanni Bellini: The Assumption of the Virgin with Saints and the painting known as the Doge Agostino Barbarigo Madonna as well as a Virgin Enthroned and Child. Paolo Veronese: St. Agatha visited in prison by St. Peter and an Angel (left aisle). **Glass Museum.** The museum's collection has recently been remounted and offers an interesting introduction to Murano glass over the centuries. **Basilica of Santi Maria e Donato**. The church was built in the 12th. century, and amongst the most interesting things to see are the outside wall of the apse, the 12th. century mosaic floors inside and the mosaic of the Virgin in the vault of the apse.

Murano Glass. The master glassmaker works his material with a long, hollow iron rod and calipers. He takes the amount of material needed from the oven - molten silica and alkalis - and twirls the rod constantly to ensure that the dense, red liquid adheres. With calipers he cuts, beats and shapes the object and opens the ball, for a vase or a glass, created by the blowing operation, which immediately opens with the rotary movement of the rod. The craftsman has little time to work the material, which he returns to the furnace frequently to keep the temperature at a suitable level for the process.

Murano, Basilica of Santi Maria e Donato

Murano glass

The Lido. The Lido, together with the other littorals which border the lagoon right down to Chioggia, is a long, narrow tongue of land formed because of the inability of the tides to wash away the silt brought down by the rivers which emptied into the sea at this point. Though these strips of land form a natural protective barrier against the violence of the sea for the city of Venice, there are points at which the littoral is so narrow that heavy seas threatened to break through. To ensure Venice's safety therefore, the government of the Republic reinforced the shores with sea-walls made of massive blocks of Istrian stone. The first point at which the Lido assumed an important place in the annals of the history of Venice was in 1202 when Doge Andrea Dandolo confined the Crusaders there, refusing to transport them to Jerusalem until they raised enough gold and silver to pay Venice for her services. It was only when the plague began to break out among the forces that the Crusaders decided to accept the conditions imposed by the Doge so they were finally able to set out on the Crusade which ended with the conquest of Constantinople. At the beginning of this century, when the Lido was still thickly wooded, the beaches there began to become fashionable and members of the Russian royal family came to spend the Winter in the great new hotels which were appearing. As the century continued the woods were cut to make way for new houses, villas and hotels. Now, the Lido beaches are still fashionable but they retain the personal character of being the Venetians' beaches too: the city transfers there in Summer and with tables, deck-chairs, cardgames and children everywhere, the days pass easily in gossip and chatter.
Malamocco, Alberoni, San Pietro in Volta and Pellestrina. Malamocco is a fishing village built after the sea had destroyed Matemaucus, one of the two political centres of the original inhabitants of the lagoon. Alberoni is a well-equipped bathing resort and also boasts a fine golf course. The name of San Pietro in Volta recalls the occasion when Pippin, the son of Charlemagne, was forced to turn back ("Volta") from his vain attempt to conquer Venice. This is a good place to see the Murazzi, the stone sea-wall erected by the authorities of the Republic a few years before the Republic itself fell in the 18th. century.

Gondola. The gondola, with its asymmetrical form - half of the stern above the surface of the water - its way of moving through the water, and the movements of the gondolier to thrust it forward and guide it, is possibly the most typical symbol of the city. The craft is a masterpiece of carpentry made up of 280 wooden parts. From its origins, it has been at the service of the nobility and used for important ceremonies, slipping through the low waters of the lagoon with ease and elegance. If architecture, sculpture and painting, with all their colours, represent Venice in a wholly special way, the gondola is the symbol of its imagination.

San Francesco del Deserto ▶

ALPHABETICAL INDEX

STORTI EDIZIONI

VENEZIA

Tel.041/431607 - Fax 041/432347
C.P. 361 30170 Mestre P.T. VE
Via Miranese, 104 La Fossa di Mirano,Venezia

Photography: Archivio Storti, Di Giovine. Printed, May 1996